D0827141

GREAT SPEECHES BY FREDERICK DOUGLASS

DOVER THRIFT EDITIONS

Edited by
James Daley

DOVER PUBLICATIONS, INC.
MINEOLA, NEW YORK

DOVER THRIFT EDITIONS

GENERAL EDITOR: MARY CAROLYN WALDREP
EDITOR OF THIS VOLUME: ALISON DAURIO

Bibliographical Note

This Dover edition, first published in 2013, is a new selection of the speeches of
Frederick Douglass made by James Daley, who also provided the Editor's Notes, as well
as the Historical Facts which precede each speech.

International Standard Book Number

ISBN-13: 978-0-486-49882-9
ISBN-10: 0-486-49882-4

Manufactured in the United States by LSC Communications
49882404   2020
www.doverpublications.com

Editor's Note

The impact of the life of Frederick Douglass on the history of American civil rights, and on the abolition of slavery, cannot be understated. After being born into slavery in Maryland in 1818, Douglass escaped his life of captivity at the age of 20 before going on to become one of the nation's leading abolitionists, activists, authors, and statesmen. During his lauded career, he wrote several autobiographies, advised presidents and politicians, and worked not only for the rights of African Americans, but for the equal treatment of women and other minority groups as well.

Despite his numerous and influential publications, Frederick Douglass was perhaps best known during his life as a consummate orator, sought out the world over to speak on behalf of African Americans and persecuted people everywhere. Spanning over a half-century of American history, his speeches, addresses, and lectures comprise a stunning account of the struggle for equality throughout the 19th century. It is the aim of this anthology to provide a glimpse into this struggle, and the man who toiled so tirelessly for its success.

Beginning in 1841, *The Church and Prejudice* survives as one of Douglass's most lasting condemnations of the hypocrisy that allowed a supposedly Christian nation to condone the abomination of slavery within its borders. His 1845 address, *My Slave Experiences in Maryland*, given just one week after completing *The Narrative of the Life of Frederick Douglass*, provides one of the first instances in which Douglass speaks publicly about his life as a slave. *Appeal to the British People, We Have Decided to Stay, What to the Slave is the 4th of July?* and *A Plea for Free Speech in Boston* trace the perils and plights of American slaves during the lead-up to the civil war, while *John Brown* and *Oration in Memory of Abraham Lincoln* discuss with great clarity the lives of two men who worked so hard for their freedom. Meanwhile, through *What the Black Man Wants, The Race Problem,* and *Lecture on Haiti*, we get a glimpse of Douglass's unceasing work to ensure full equality, both at home and abroad, for African Americans and all freed slaves in the wake of their emancipation.

Finally, in what is perhaps his most passionate and inspirational address, we come to Douglass's famed *Self-Made Men*. Given many times in numerous venues throughout his life, this speech serves as a lasting call to arms of all people born into lowly means to rise above their meager circumstances, and build a better life through dedication, education, and hard work. The version of this speech included in the present anthology was the last one Douglass gave, delivered just 10 months before his death. In it, he extols the virtues and qualities of "Self-Made Men" and makes a particular point to describe America as a unique and vital land of opportunity, which, if equal rights are truly achieved by all, can reach its greatest potential: not to become a nation that hands its citizens an equal share of wealth and riches, but a country where all citizens are given an equal chance to achieve greatness on their own.

In his own words:

> We have as a people no past and very little present, but a boundless and glorious future. With us, it is not so much what has been, or what is now, but what is to be in the good time coming. Our mottoes are "Look ahead!" and "Go ahead!," and especially the latter. Our moral atmosphere is full of the inspiration of hope and courage. Every man has his chance. If he cannot be President he can, at least, be prosperous. In this respect, America is not only the exception to the general rule, but the social wonder of the world. . . . These causes which make America the home and foster-mother of self-made men, combined with universal suffrage, will, I hope, preserve us from . . . danger. With equal suffrage in our hands, we are beyond the power of families, nationalities, or races. Then, too, our national genius welcomes humanity from every quarter and grants to all an equal chance in the race of life.

It is with this sentiment that Frederick Douglass's words live on as powerful and pertinent today as they were in his own lifetime. While we may have won an end to slavery, universal suffrage, and countless other civil rights battles, there is no doubt that were he still alive today, Frederick Douglass would be speaking and struggling to attain the true freedom and fairness necessary for all men and women, regardless of race, nationality, gender, sexual orientation or income, to be given an "equal chance in the race of life."

—James Daley
Editor

Contents

Contents

The Church and Prejudice
(1841)

*In this speech, delivered two decades before the beginning of the Civil War,
Douglass describes the hypocrisy often seen at the time in Christian churches
throughout the country, wherein many African Americans were not treated the
same as whites. It was delivered on November 4, 1841 before the Plymouth
County Anti-Slavery Society, in Plymouth, Massachusetts.*

At the South I was a member of the Methodist Church. When I came
north, I thought one Sunday I would attend communion, at one of
the churches of my denomination, in the town I was staying. The
white people gathered round the altar, the blacks clustered by the door.
After the good minister had served out the bread and wine to one
portion of those near him, he said, "These may withdraw, and others
come forward;" thus he proceeded till all the white members had been
served. Then he took a long breath, and looking out towards the door,
exclaimed, "Come up, colored friends, come up! for you know God
is no respecter of persons!" I haven't been there to see the sacraments
taken since.

At New Bedford, where I live, there was a great revival of religion
not long ago—many were converted and "received" as they said, "into
the kingdom of heaven." But it seems, the kingdom of heaven is like a
net; at least so it was according to the practice of these pious Christians;
and when the net was drawn ashore, they had to set down and cull out
the fish. Well, it happened now that some of the fish had rather black
scales; so these were sorted out and packed by themselves. But among
those who experienced religion at this time was a colored girl; she was
baptized in the same water as the rest; so she thought she might sit at
the Lord's table and partake of the same sacramental elements with the
others. The deacon handed round the cup, and when he came to the
black girl, he could not pass her, for there was the minister looking
right at him, and as he was a kind of abolitionist, the deacon was rather
afraid of giving him offense; so he handed the girl the cup, and she

tasted. Now it so happened that next to her sat a young lady who had been converted at the same time, baptized in the same water, and put her trust in the same blessed Savior; yet when the cup containing the precious blood which had been shed for all, came to her, she rose in disdain, and walked out of the church. Such was the religion she had experienced!

Another young lady fell into a trance. When she awoke, she declared she had been to heaven. Her friends were all anxious to know what and whom she had seen there; so she told the whole story. But there was one good old lady whose curiosity went beyond that of all the others—and she inquired of the girl that had the vision, if she saw any black folks in heaven? After some hesitation, the reply was, "Oh! I didn't go into the kitchen!"

Thus you see, my hearers, this prejudice goes even into the church of God. And there are those who carry it so far that it is disagreeable to them even to think of going to heaven, if colored people are going there too. And whence comes it? The grand cause is slavery; but there are others less prominent; one of them is the way in which children in this part of the country are instructed to regard the blacks.

"Yes!" exclaimed an old gentleman, interrupting him—"when they behave wrong, they are told, 'black man come catch you.'"

Yet people in general will say they like colored men as well as any other, but in their proper place! They assign us that place; they don't let us do it for ourselves, nor will they allow us a voice in the decision. They will not allow that we have a head to think, and a heart to feel, and a soul to aspire. They treat us not as men, but as dogs—they cry "Stu-boy!" and expect us to run and do their bidding. That's the way we are liked. You degrade us, and then ask why we are degraded—you shut our mouths, and then ask why we don't speak—you close our colleges and seminaries against us, and then ask why we don't know more.

But all this prejudice sinks into insignificance in my mind, when compared with the enormous iniquity of the system which is its cause—the system that sold my four sisters and my brothers into bondage—and which calls in its priests to defend it even from the Bible! The slaveholding ministers preach up the divine right of the slaveholders to property in their fellow men. The southern preachers say to the poor slave, "Oh! if you wish to be happy in time, happy in eternity, you must be obedient to your masters; their interest is yours. God made one portion of men to do the working, and another to do the thinking; how good God is! Now, you have no trouble or anxiety; but ah! you can't imagine how perplexing it is to your masters and mistresses to have so much thinking to do in your behalf! You cannot appreciate your blessings; you know not how happy a thing it is for you, that you were born of that portion of the human family which has the working, instead of the thinking to do! Oh! how grateful and obedient you ought to be to your masters! How beautiful are the arrangements of Providence! Look at your hard, horny hands—see how nicely they are adapted to the labor you have to perform! Look at our delicate fingers, so exactly fitted for our station, and see how manifest it is that God designed us to be His thinkers, and you the workers—Oh! the wisdom of God!" I used to attend a Methodist church, in which my master was a class leader; he would talk most sanctimoniously about the dear Redeemer, who was sent "to preach deliverance to the captives, and set at liberty them that are bruised"—he could pray at morning, pray at noon, and pray at night; yet he could lash up my poor cousin by his two thumbs, and inflict stripes and blows upon his bare back, till the blood streamed to the ground! all the time quoting scripture, for his authority, and ap-pealing to that passage of the Holy Bible which says, "He that knoweth his master's will, and doeth it not, shall be beaten with many stripes!" Such was the amount of this good Methodist's piety.

My Slave Experience in Maryland
(1845)

On May 6, 1845, Frederick Douglass gave the following address before the American Anti-Slavery Society in New York City, just one week after completing work on his autobiography, The Narrative of Frederick Douglass. *It is widely believed to be the first public address in which Douglass speaks in great detail about his personal experiences as a slave.*

I do not know that I can say anything to the point. My habits and early life have done much to unfit me for public speaking, and I fear that your patience has already been wearied by the lengthened remarks of other speakers, more eloquent than I can possibly be, and better prepared to command the attention of the audience. And I can scarcely hope to get your attention even for a longer period than fifteen minutes.

Before coming to this meeting, I had a sort of desire I don't know but it was vanity to stand before a New York audience in the Tabernacle. But when I came in this morning, and looked at those massive pillars, and saw the vast throng which had assembled, I got a little frightened, and was afraid that I could not speak; but now that the audience is not so large and I have recovered from my fright, I will venture to say a word on Slavery.

I ran away from the South seven years ago passing through this city in no little hurry, I assure you and lived about three years in New Bedford, Massachusetts, before I became publicly known to the anti-slavery people. Since then I have been engaged for three years in telling the people what I know of it. I have come to this meeting to throw in my mite, and since no fugitive slave has preceded me, I am encouraged to say a word about the sunny South. I thought, when the eloquent female who addressed this audience a while ago, was speaking of the horrors of Slavery, that many an honest man would doubt the truth of the picture which she drew; and I can unite with the gentleman from Kentucky in saying, that she came far short of describing them.

I can tell you what I have seen with my own eyes, felt on my own person, and know to have occurred in my own neighborhood. I am not from any of those States where the slaves are said to be in their most degraded condition; but from Maryland, where Slavery is said to exist in its mildest form; yet I can stand here and relate atrocities which would make your blood to boil at the statement of them. I lived on the plantation of Col. Lloyd, on the eastern shore of Maryland, and belonged to that gentleman's clerk. He owned, probably, not less than a thousand slaves.

I mention the name of this man, and also of the persons who perpetrated the deeds which I am about to relate, running the risk of being hurled back into interminable bondage for I am yet a slave; yet for the sake of the cause for the sake of humanity, I will mention the names, and glory in running the risk. I have the gratification to know that if I fall by the utterance of truth in this matter, that if I shall be hurled back into bondage to gratify the slaveholder to be killed by inches that every drop of blood which I shall shed, every groan which I shall utter, every pain which shall rack my frame, every sob in which I shall indulge, shall be the instrument, under God, of tearing down the bloody pillar of Slavery, and of hastening the day of deliverance for three millions of my brethren in bondage.

I therefore tell the names of these bloody men, not because they are worse than other men would have been in their circumstances. No, they are bloody from necessity. Slavery makes it necessary for the slaveholder to commit all conceivable outrages upon the miserable slave. It is impossible to hold the slaves in bondage without this.

We had on the plantation an overseer, by the name of Austin Gore, a man who was highly respected as an overseer proud, ambitious, cruel, artful, obdurate. Nearly every slave stood in the utmost dread and horror of that man. His eye flashed confusion amongst them. He never spoke but to command, nor commanded but to be obeyed. He was lavish with the whip, sparing with his word. I have seen that man tie up men by the two hands, and for two hours, at intervals, ply the lash. I have seen women stretched up on the limbs of trees, and their bare backs made bloody with the lash. One slave refused to be whipped by him I need not tell you that he was a man, though black his features, degraded his condition. He had committed some trifling offence for they whip for trifling offences. The slave refused to be whipped, and ran. He did not stand to and fight his master as I did once, and might do again though I hope I shall not have occasion to do so. He ran and stood in a creek, and refused to come out. At length his master told him he would shoot him if he did not come out. Three calls were to be given him. The first, second, and third, were given, at each of which the slave stood his ground. Gore, equally determined and firm, raised his musket, and in an instant poor Derby was no more. He sank beneath the waves, and naught but the crimsoned waters marked the spot. Then a general outcry might be heard amongst us. Mr. Lloyd asked Gore why he had resorted to such a cruel measure. He replied, coolly, that he had done it from necessity; that the slave was setting a dangerous example, and that if he was permitted to be corrected and yet save his life, that the slaves would effectually rise and be freemen, and their masters be slaves. His defense was satisfactory. He remained on the plantation, and his fame went abroad. He still lives in St. Michaels, Talbot County, Maryland, and is now, I presume, as much respected, as though his guilty soul had never been stained with his brother's blood.

I might go on and mention other facts if time would permit. My own wife had a dear cousin who was terribly mangled in her sleep, while nursing the child of a Mrs. Hicks. Finding the girl asleep, Mrs. Hicks beat her to death with a billet of wood, and the woman has never been brought to justice. It is not a crime to kill a Negro in Talbot county, Maryland, farther than it is a deprivation of a man's property. I used to know of one who boasted that he had killed two slaves, and with an oath would say, "I'm the only benefactor in the country."

Now, my friends, pardon me for having detained you so long; but let me tell you with regard to the feelings of the slave. The people at the North say "Why don't you rise? If we were thus treated we would rise and throw off the yoke. We would wade knee deep in blood before we would endure the bondage." You'd rise up! Who are these that are asking for manhood in the slave, and who say that he has it not, because he does not rise? The very men who are ready by the Constitution to bring the strength of the nation to put us down! You, the people of New York, the people of Massachusetts, of New England, of the whole Northern States, have sworn under God that we shall be slaves or die! And shall we three millions be taunted with a want of the love of freedom, by the very men who stand upon us and say, submit, or be crushed?

We don't ask you to engage in any physical warfare against the slaveholder. We only ask that in Massachusetts, and the several non-slaveholding States which maintain a union with the slaveholder who stand with your heavy heels on the quivering heart strings of the slave, that you will stand off. Leave us to take care of our masters. But here you come up to our masters and tell them that they ought to shoot us to take away our wives and little ones to sell our mothers into interminable bondage, and sever the tenderest ties. You say to us, if you dare to carry out the principles of our fathers, we'll shoot you down.

Others may tamely submit; not I. You may put the chains upon me and fetter me, but I am not a slave, for my master who puts the chains upon me, shall stand in as much dread of me as I do of him. I ask you in the name of my three millions of brethren at the South. We know that we are unable to cope with you in numbers; you are numerically stronger, politically stronger, than we are but we ask you if you will rend asunder the heart and [crush] the body of the slave? If so, you must do it at your own expense.

While you continue in the Union, you are as bad as the slaveholder. If you have thus wronged the poor black man, by stripping him of his freedom, how are you going to give evidence of your repentance? Undo what you have done. Do you say that the slave ought not to be free? These hands are they not mine? This body is it not mine? Again, I am your brother, white as you are. I'm your blood kin. You don't get rid of me so easily. I mean to hold on to you. And in this land of liberty, I'm a slave. The twenty-six States that blaze forth on your flag, proclaim a compact to return me to bondage if I run away, and keep me in bondage if I submit. Wherever I go, under the aegis of your liberty, there I'm a slave. If I go to Lexington or Bunker Hill, there I'm a slave, chained in perpetual servitude. I may go to your deepest valley, to your highest mountain, I'm still a slave, and the bloodhound may chase me down.

Now I ask you if you are willing to have your country the hunting ground of the slave. God says thou shalt not oppress; the Constitution says oppress; which will you serve, God or man? The American Anti-Slavery Society says God, and I am thankful for it. In the name of my brethren, to you, Mr. President, and the noble band who cluster around you, to you, who are scouted on every hand by priest, people, politician, Church, and State, to you I bring a thankful heart, and in the name of three millions of slaves, I offer you their gratitude for your faithful advocacy in behalf of the slave.

Appeal to the British People
(1846)

From summer of 1845 until the spring of 1847, Fredrick Douglass spent the better part of two years touring Ireland and England, speaking at churches and public meetings about the horrors of slavery in the United States of America. While he was well received almost everywhere he traveled, his most influential speech from this trip was undoubtedly the following, which he gave at London's Finsbury Chapel on May 12, 1846.

I feel exceedingly glad of the opportunity now afforded me of presenting the claims of my brethren in bonds in the United States, to so many in London and from various parts of Britain, who have assembled here on the present occasion. I have nothing to commend me to your consideration in the way of learning, nothing in the way of education, to entitle me to your attention; and you are aware that slavery is a very bad school for rearing teachers of morality and religion. Twenty-one years of my life have been spent in slavery—personal slavery—surrounded by degrading influences, such as can exist nowhere beyond the pale of slavery; and it will not be strange, if under such circumstances, I should betray, in what I have to say to you, a deficiency of that refinement which is seldom or ever found, except among persons that have experienced superior advantages to those which I have enjoyed. But I will take it for granted that you know something about the degrading influences of slavery, and that you will not expect great things from me this evening, but simply such facts as I may be able to advance immediately in connection with my own experience of slavery.

Now what is this system of slavery? This is the subject of my lecture this evening—what is the character of this institution? I am about to answer the inquiry, what is American slavery? I do this the more readily, since I have found persons in this country who have identified the term slavery with that which I think it is not, and in some instances, I have feared, in so doing, have rather (unwittingly, I know) detracted much from the horror with which the term slavery is contemplated. It is common in this country to distinguish every bad thing by the name of slavery. Intemperance is slavery; to be deprived of the right to vote is slavery, says one; to have to work hard is slavery, says another; and I do not know but that if we should let them go on, they would say that to eat when we are hungry, to walk when we desire to have exercise, or to minister to our necessities, or have necessities at all, is slavery. I do not wish for a moment to detract from the horror with which the evil of intemperance is contemplated—not at all; nor do I wish to throw the slightest obstruction in the way of any political freedom that any class of persons in this country may desire to obtain. But I am here to say that I think the term slavery is sometimes abused by identifying it with that which it is not. Slavery in the United States is the granting of that power by which one man exercises and enforces a right of property in the body and soul of another. The condition of a slave is simply that of the brute beast. He is a piece of property—a marketable commodity, in the language of the law, to be bought or sold at the will and caprice of the master who claims him to be his property; he is spoken of, thought of, and treated as property. His own good, his conscience, his intellect, his affections, are all set aside by the master. The will and the wishes of the master are the law of the slave. He is as much a piece of property as a horse. If he is fed, he is fed because he is property. If he is clothed, it is with a view to the increase of his value as property. Whatever of comfort is necessary to him for his body or soul that is inconsistent with his being property, is carefully wrested from him, not only by public opinion, but by the law of the country. He is carefully deprived of everything that tends in the slightest degree to detract from his value as property. He is deprived of education. God has given him an intellect; the slaveholder declares it shall not be cultivated. If his moral perception leads him in a course contrary to his value as property, the slaveholder declares he shall not exercise it. The marriage institution cannot exist among slaves, and one-sixth of the population of democratic America is denied its privileges by the law of the land. What is to be thought of a nation boasting of its liberty, boasting of its humanity, boasting of its Christianity, boasting of its love of justice and purity, and yet having within its own borders three millions of persons denied by law the right of marriage?—what must be the condition of that people? I need not lift up the veil by giving you any experience of my own. Everyone that can put two ideas together, must see the most fearful results from such a state of things as I have just mentioned. If any of these three millions find for themselves companions, and prove themselves honest, upright, virtuous persons to each other, yet in these cases—few as I am bound to confess they are—the virtuous live in constant apprehension of being torn asunder by the merciless menstealers that claim them as their property. This is American slavery; no marriage—no education—the light of the gospel shut out from the dark mind of the bondman—and he forbidden by law to learn to read. If a mother shall teach her children to read, the law in Louisiana proclaims that she may be hanged by the neck. If the father attempt to give his son a knowledge of letters, he may be punished by the whip in one instance, and in another be killed, at the discretion of the court. Three millions of people shut out from the light of knowledge! It is easy for you to conceive the evil that must result from such a state of things.

I now come to the physical evils of slavery. I do not wish to dwell at length upon these, but it seems right to speak of them, not so much to influence your minds on this question, as to let the slaveholders of America know that the curtain which conceals their crimes is being lifted abroad; that we are opening the dark cell, and leading the people into the horrible recesses of what they are pleased to call their domestic institution. We want them to know that a knowledge of their whippings, their scourgings, their brandings, their chainings, is not confined to their plantations, but that some Negro of theirs has broken loose from his chains—has burst through the dark incrustation of slavery, and is now exposing their deeds of deep damnation to the gaze of the Christian people of England.

The slaveholders resort to all kinds of cruelty. If I were disposed, I have matter enough to interest you on this question for five or six evenings, but I will not dwell at length upon these cruelties. Suffice it to say, that all of the peculiar modes of torture that were resorted to in the West India islands, are resorted to, I believe, even more frequently, in the United States of America. Starvation, the bloody whip, the chain, the gag, the thumb-screw, cat-hauling, the cat-o'-nine-tails, the dungeon, the blood-hound, are all in requisition to keep the slave in his condition as a slave in the United States. If any one has a doubt upon this point, I would ask him to read the chapter on slavery in Dickens's *Notes on America*. If any man has a doubt upon it, I have here the "testimony of a thousand witnesses," which I can give at any length, all going to prove the truth of my statement. The blood-hound is regularly trained in the United States, and advertisements are to be found in the southern papers of the Union, from persons advertising themselves as blood-hound trainers, and offering to hunt down slaves at fifteen dollars a piece, recommending their hounds as the fleetest in the neighborhood, never known to fail. Advertisements are from time to time inserted, stating that slaves have escaped with iron collars about their necks, with bands of iron about their feet, marked with the lash, branded with red-hot irons, the initials of their master's name burned into their flesh; and the masters advertise the fact of their being thus branded with their own signature, thereby proving to the world, that, however damning it may appear to non-slavers, such practices are not regarded discreditable among the slaveholders themselves. Why, I believe if a man should brand his horse in this country—burn the initials of his name into any of his cattle, and publish the ferocious deed here—that the united execrations of Christians in Britain would descend upon him. Yet in the United States, human beings are thus branded. As Whittier says—

... Our countrymen in chains,
The whip on woman's shrinking flesh,
Our soil yet reddening with the stains
Caught from her scourgings warm and fresh.

The slave-dealer boldly publishes his infamous acts to the world. Of all things that have been said of slavery to which exception has been taken by slaveholders, this, the charge of cruelty, stands foremost, and yet there is no charge capable of clearer demonstration, than that of the most barbarous inhumanity on the part of the slaveholders toward their slaves. And all this is necessary; it is necessary to resort to these cruelties, in order to make the slave a slave, and to keep him a slave. Why, my experience all goes to prove the truth of what you will call a marvelous proposition, that the better you treat a slave, the more you destroy his value as a slave, and enhance the probability of his eluding the grasp of the slaveholder; the more kindly you treat him, the more wretched you make him, while you keep him in the condition of a slave. My experience, I say, confirms the truth of this proposition. When I was treated exceedingly ill; when my back was being scourged daily; when I was whipped within an inch of my life—life was all I cared for. "Spare my life," was my continual prayer. When I was looking for the blow about to be inflicted upon my head, I was not thinking of my liberty; it was my life. But, as soon as the blow was not to be feared, then came the longing for liberty. If a slave has a bad master, his ambition is to get a better; when he gets a better, he aspires to have the best; and when he gets the best, he aspires to be his own master. But the slave must be brutalized to keep him as a slave. The slaveholder feels this necessity. I admit this necessity. If it be right to hold slaves at all, it is right to hold them in the only way in which they can be held; and this can be done only by shutting out the light of education from their minds, and brutalizing their persons. The whip, the chain, the gag, the thumb-screw, the blood-hound, the stocks, and all the other bloody paraphernalia of the slave system, are indispensably necessary to the relation of master and slave. The slave must be subjected to these, or he ceases to be a slave. Let him know that the whip is burned; that the fetters have been turned to some useful and profitable employment; that the chain is no longer for his limbs; that the blood-hound is no longer to be put upon his track; that his master's authority over him is no longer to be enforced by taking his life—and immediately he walks out from the house of bondage and asserts his freedom as a man. The slaveholder finds it necessary to have these implements to keep the slave in bondage; finds it necessary to be able to say, "Unless you do so and so; Unless you do as I bid you—I will take away your life!"

Some of the most awful scenes of cruelty are constantly taking place in the middle states of the Union. We have in those states what are called the slave-breeding states. Allow me to speak plainly. Although it is harrowing to your feelings, it is necessary that the facts of the case should be stated. We have in the United States slave-breeding states. The very state from which the minister from our court to yours comes, is one of these states—Maryland, where men, women, and children are reared for the market, just as horses, sheep, and swine are raised for the market. Slave-rearing is there looked upon as a legitimate trade; the law sanctions it, public opinion upholds it, the church does not condemn it. It goes on in all its bloody horrors, sustained by the auctioneer's block. If you would see the cruelties of this system, hear the following narrative. Not long since the following scene occurred. A slave-woman and a slave-man had united themselves as man and wife in the absence of any law to protect them as man and wife. They had lived together by the permission, not by right, of their master, and they had reared a family. The master found it expedient, and for his interest, to sell them. He did not ask them their wishes in regard to the matter at all; they were not consulted. The man and woman were brought to the auctioneer's block, under the sound of the hammer. The cry was raised, "Here goes; who bids cash?" Think of it—a man and wife to be sold! The woman was placed on the auctioneer's block; her limbs, as is customary, were brutally exposed to the purchasers, who examined her with all the freedom with which they would examine a horse. There stood the husband, powerless; no right to his wife; the master's right preeminent. She was sold. He was next brought to the auctioneer's block. His eyes followed his wife in the distance; and he looked beseechingly, imploringly, to the man that had bought his wife, to buy him also. But he was at length bid off to another person. He was about to be separated forever from her he loved. No word of his, no work of his, could save him from this separation. He asked permission of his new master to go and take the hand of his wife at parting. It was denied him. In the agony of his soul he rushed from the man who had just bought him, that he might take a farewell of his wife; but his way was obstructed, he was struck over the head with a loaded whip, and was held for a moment; but his agony was too great. When he was let go, he fell a corpse at the feet of his master. His heart was broken. Such scenes are the everyday fruits of American slavery. Some two years since, the Hon. Seth. M. Gates, an anti-slavery gentleman of the state of New York, a representative in the congress of the United States, told me he saw with his own eyes the following circumstances. In the national District of Columbia, over which the star-spangled emblem is constantly waving, where orators are ever holding forth on the subject of American liberty, American democracy, American republicanism, there are two slave prisons. When going across a bridge, leading to one of these prisons, he saw a young woman run out, bare-footed and bare-headed, and with very little clothing on. She was running with all speed to the bridge he was approaching. His eye was fixed upon her, and he stopped to see what was the matter. He had not paused long before he saw three men run out after her. He now knew what the nature of the case was; a slave escaping from her chains—a young woman, a sister—escaping from the bondage in which she had been held. She made her way to the bridge, but had not reached, ere from the Virginia side there came two slaveholders. As soon as they saw them, her pursuers called out, "Stop her!" True to their Virginian instincts, they came to the rescue of their brother kidnappers, across the bridge. The poor girl now saw that there was no chance for her. It was a trying time. She knew if she went back, she must be a slave forever—she must be dragged down to the scenes of pollution which the slaveholders continually provide for most of the poor, sinking, wretched young women, whom they call their property. She formed her resolution; and just as those who were about to take her, were going to put hands upon her, to drag her back, she leaped over the balustrades of the bridge, and down she went to rise no more. She chose death, rather than to go back into the hands of those Christian slaveholders from whom she had escaped.

Can it be possible that such things as these exist in the United States? Are not these the exceptions? Are any such scenes as this general? Are not such deeds condemned by the law and denounced by public opinion? Let me read to you a few of the laws of the slaveholding states of America. I think no better exposure of slavery can be made than is made by the laws of the states in which slavery exists. I prefer reading the laws to making any statement in confirmation of what I have said myself; for the slaveholders cannot object to this testimony, since it is the calm, the cool, the deliberate enactment of their wisest heads, of their most clear-sighted, their own constituted representatives. "If more than seven slaves together are found in any road without a white person, twenty lashes a piece; for visiting a plantation without a written pass, ten lashes; for letting loose a boat from where it is made fast, thirty-nine lashes for the first offense; and for the second, shall have cut off from his head one ear; for keeping or carrying a club, thirty-nine lashes; for having any article for sale, without a ticket from his master, ten lashes; for traveling in any other than the most usual and accustomed road, when going alone to any place, forty lashes; for traveling in the night without a pass, forty lashes." I am afraid you do not understand the awful character of these lashes. You must bring it before your mind. A human being in a perfect state of nudity, tied hand and foot to a stake, and a strong man standing behind with a heavy whip, knotted at the end, each blow cutting into the flesh, and leaving the warm blood dripping to the feet; and for these trifles. "For being found in another person's Negro-quarters, forty lashes; for hunting with dogs in the woods, thirty lashes; for being on horseback without the written permission of his master, twenty-five lashes; for riding or going abroad in the night, or riding horses in the day time, without leave, a slave may be whipped, cropped, or branded in the cheek with the letter R. or otherwise punished, such punishment not extending to life, or so as to render him unfit for labor." The laws referred to, may be found by consulting *Brevard's Digest*; *Haywood's Manual*; *Virginia Revised Code*; *Prince's Digest*; *Missouri Laws*; *Mississippi Revised Code*. A man, for going to visit his brethren, without the permission of his master—and in many instances he may not have that permission; his master, from caprice or other reasons, may not be willing to allow it—may be caught on his way, dragged to a post, the branding-iron heated, and the name of his master or the letter R branded into his cheek or on his forehead. They treat slaves thus, on the principle that they must punish for light offenses, in order to prevent the commission of larger ones. I wish you to mark that in the single state of Virginia there are seventy-one crimes for which a colored man may be executed; while there are only three of these crimes, which, when committed by a white man, will subject him to that punishment. There are many of these crimes which if the white man did not commit, he would be regarded as a scoundrel and a coward. In the state of Maryland, there is a law to this effect: that if a slave shall strike his master, he may be hanged, his head severed from his body, his body quartered, and his head and quarters set up in the most prominent places in the neighborhood. If a colored woman, in the defense of her own virtue, in defense of her own person, should shield herself from the brutal attacks of her tyrannical master, or make the slightest resistance, she may be killed on the spot. No law whatever will bring the guilty man to justice for the crime.

But you will ask me, can these things be possible in a land professing Christianity? Yes, they are so; and this is not the worst. No; a darker feature is yet to be presented than the mere existence of these facts. I have to inform you that the religion of the southern states, at this time, is the great supporter, the great sanctioner of the bloody atrocities to which I have referred. While America is printing tracts and bibles; sending missionaries abroad to convert the heathen; expending her money in various ways for the promotion of the gospel in foreign lands—the slave not only lies forgotten, uncared for, but is trampled under foot by the very churches of the land. What have we in America? Why, we have slavery made part of the religion of the land. Yes, the pulpit there stands up as the great defender of this cursed institution, as it is called. Ministers of religion come forward and torture the hallowed pages of inspired wisdom to sanction the bloody deed. They stand forth as the foremost, the strongest defenders of this "institution." As a proof of this, I need not do more than state the general fact, that slavery has existed under the droppings of the sanctuary of the south for the last two hundred years, and there has not been any war between the religion and the slavery of the south. Whips, chains, gags, and thumb-screws have all lain under the droppings of the sanctuary, and instead of rusting from off the limbs of the bondman, those droppings have served to preserve them in all their strength. Instead of preaching the gospel against this tyranny, rebuke, and wrong, ministers of religion have sought, by all and every means, to throw in the back-ground whatever in the bible could be construed into opposition to slavery, and to bring forward that which they could torture into its support. This I conceive to be the darkest feature of slavery, and the most difficult to attack, because it is identified with religion, and exposes those who denounce it to the charge of infidelity. Yes, those with whom I have been laboring, namely, the old organization anti-slavery society of America, have been again and again stigmatized as infidels, and for what reason? Why, solely in consequence of the faithfulness of their attacks upon the slaveholding religion of the southern states, and the northern religion that sympathizes with it. I have found it difficult to speak on this matter without persons coming forward and saying, "Douglass, are you not afraid of injuring the cause of Christ? You do not desire to do so, we know; but are you not undermining religion?" This has been said to me again and again, even since I came to this country, but I cannot be induced to leave off these exposures. I love the religion of our blessed Savior. I love that religion that comes from above, in the "wisdom of God," which is first pure, then peaceable, gentle, and easy to be entreated, full of mercy and good fruits, without partiality and without hypocrisy. I love that religion that sends its votaries to bind up the wounds of him that has fallen among thieves. I love that religion that makes it the duty of its disciples to visit the father less and the widow in their affliction. I love that religion that is based upon the glorious principle, of love to God and love to man;

which makes its followers do unto others as they themselves would be done by. If you demand liberty to yourself, it says, grant it to your neighbors. If you claim a right to think for yourself, it says, allow your neighbors the same right. If you claim to act for yourself, it says, allow your neighbors the same right. It is because I love this religion that I hate the slaveholding, the woman-whipping, the mind-darkening, the soul-destroying religion that exists in the southern states of America. It is because I regard the one as good, and pure, and holy, that I cannot but regard the other as bad, corrupt, and wicked. Loving the one I must hate the other; holding to the one I must reject the other.

I may be asked, why I am so anxious to bring this subject before the British public—why I do not confine my efforts to the United States? My answer is, first, that slavery is the common enemy of mankind, and all mankind should be made acquainted with its abominable character. My next answer is, that the slave is a man, and, as such, is entitled to your sympathy as a brother. All the feelings, all the susceptibilities, all the capacities, which you have, he has. He is a part of the human family. He has been the prey—the common prey—of Christendom for the last three hundred years, and it is but right, it is but just, it is but proper, that his wrongs should be known throughout the world. I have another reason for bringing this matter before the British public, and it is this: slavery is a system of wrong, so blinding to all around, so hardening to the heart, so corrupting to the morals, so deleterious to religion, so sapping to all the principles of justice in its immediate vicinity, that the community surrounding it lacks the moral stamina necessary to its removal. It is a system of such gigantic evil, so strong, so overwhelming in its power, that no one nation is equal to its removal. It requires the humanity of Christianity, the morality of the world to remove it. Hence, I call upon the people of Britain to look at this matter, and to exert the influence I am about to show they possess, for the removal of slavery from America. I can appeal to them, as strongly by their regard for the slaveholder as for the slave, to labor in this cause. I am here, because you have an influence on America that no other nation can have. You have been drawn together by the power of steam to a marvelous extent; the distance between London and Boston is now reduced to some twelve or fourteen days, so that the denunciations against slavery, uttered in London this week, may be heard in a fortnight in the streets of Boston, and reverberating amidst the hills of Massachusetts. There is nothing said here against slavery that will not be recorded in the United States. I am here, also, because the slaveholders do not want me to be here; they would rather that I were not here. I have adopted a maxim laid down by Napoleon, never to occupy ground which the enemy would like me to occupy. The slaveholders would much rather have me, if I will denounce slavery, denounce it in the northern states, where their friends and supporters are, who will stand by and mob me for denouncing it. They feel something as the man felt, when he uttered his prayer, in which he made out a most horrible case for himself, and one of his neighbors touched him and said, "My friend, I always had the opinion of you that you have now expressed for yourself—that you are a very great sinner." Coming from himself, it was all very well, but coming from a stranger it was rather cutting. The slaveholders felt that when slavery was denounced among themselves, it was not so bad; but let one of the slaves get loose, let him summon the people of Britain, and make known to them the conduct of the slaveholders toward their slaves, and it cuts them to the quick, and produces a sensation such as would be produced by nothing else. The power I exert now is something like the power that is exerted by the man at the end of the lever; my influence now is just in proportion to the distance that I am from the United States. My exposure of slavery abroad will tell more upon the hearts and consciences of slaveholders, than if I was attacking them in America; for almost every paper that I now receive from the United States, comes teeming with statements about this fugitive Negro, calling him a "glib-tongued scoundrel," and saying that he is running out against the institutions and people of America. I deny the charge that I am saying a word against the institutions of America, or the people, as such. What I have to say is against slavery and slaveholders. I feel at liberty to speak on this subject. I have on my back the marks of the lash; I have four sisters and one brother now under the galling chain. I feel it my duty to cry aloud and spare not. I am not averse to having the good opinion of my fellow creatures. I am not averse to being kindly regarded by all men; but I am bound, even at the hazard of making a large class of religionists in this country hate me, oppose me, and malign me as they have done—I am bound by the prayers, and tears, and entreaties of three millions of kneeling bondsmen, to have no compromise with men who are in any shape or form connected with the slaveholders of America. I expose slavery in this country, because to expose it is to kill it. Slavery is one of those monsters of darkness to whom the light of truth is death. Expose slavery, and it dies. Light is to slavery what the heat of the sun is to the root of a tree; it must die under it. All the slaveholder asks of me is silence. He does not ask me to go abroad and preach in favor of slavery; he does not ask any one to do that. He would not say that slavery is a good thing, but the best under the circumstances. The slaveholders want total darkness on the subject. They want the hatchway shut down, that the monster may crawl in his den of darkness, crushing human hopes and happiness, destroying the bondman at will, and having no one to reprove or rebuke

him. Slavery shrinks from the light; it hateth the light, neither cometh
to the light, lest its deeds should be reproved. To tear off the mask from
this abominable system, to expose it to the light of heaven, aye, to the
heat of the sun, that it may burn and wither it out of existence, is my
object in coming to this country. I want the slaveholder surrounded,
as by a wall of anti-slavery fire, so that he may see the condemnation
of himself and his system glaring down in letters of light. I want him
to feel that he has no sympathy in England, Scotland, or Ireland; that
he has none in Canada, none in Mexico, none among the poor wild
Indians; that the voice of the civilized, aye, and savage world is against
him. I would have condemnation blaze down upon him in every direction, till, stunned and overwhelmed with shame and confusion, he is
compelled to let go the grasp he holds upon the persons of his victims,
and restore them to their long-lost rights.

We Have Decided to Stay
(1848)

In this speech, Frederick Douglass addresses the policy of "Colonization" supported by many anti-slavery Americans (including, and especially, Abraham Lincoln) in which freed slaves would be voluntarily returned to Africa. It was delivered before the American Anti-Slavery Society in New York City on May 9, 1848.

Mr. Chairman, and Ladies, and Gentlemen.

It is with great hesitation that I consent to rise here to speak, after the able speech to which you have just listened. I had far rather remain a listener to others, than to become myself a speaker at this stage of the proceedings of this meeting. I do not hope to be able, in the few remarks I have to make, to say anything new or eloquent, for it will be time indeed to discuss new truths, when old ones shall have been recognized and adopted.

For seventeen years, Mr. Chairman, the Abolitionists of the United States have been encountering obloquy, scorn, and opposition of the most furious character, for uttering,—what? Their conviction that a man is a man,—that every man belongs to himself and to no one else. In propagating this idea, this simple proposition, we have met with all sorts of opposition, and with all sorts of arguments drawn from the Bible, from the Constitution, and from philosophy, till at length many have arrived at the sage conclusion that a man is something else than a man, and that he has not the rights of a man.

An event has just occurred in the District of Columbia, the Capitol of the country, known to you all, which furnishes the proof of this assertion. Some seventy-seven men, women, and children, took it into their heads, contrary to the Constitution, that they were men, not three-fifths of men—that they would leave the refined avocation of blacking boots for nothing for members of Congress, and seek an asylum from oppression and tyranny in some of the Northern States, or under the protection of the British Lion in Canada. The sequel is well

19

known; they were pursued by a band of armed men, overtaken, and brought back in chains, and the men who aided them in their flight are in a dungeon, and there they will probably end their lives.

Very little is thought about this affair,—very little noise is made about it. It excites about as much remark, and about as much sympathy as if as many horses had broken away from the halters of their owners, and again been recovered.

* * *

Sir, we have, in this country, no adequate idea of humanity yet; the nation does not feel that these are men, it cannot see through the dark skin and curly hair of the black man, anything like humanity, or that has claims to human rights. Had they been white men and women, or were they regarded as human beings, this nation would have been agitated to its centre, and rocked as with an earthquake shock, and like the nations of the Old World, would have rung with the thunders of freedom against tyranny, at such an event as this.

We do not regard these men as formed in the image of God. We do not see that in the persons of these men and women whose rights have been stricken down, whose virtuous attempt to gain their freedom, has been defeated, the violation of the common rights of man.

Even the gallant Hale, of the Liberty party, does not dare to speak of the men who aided their escape, as having done a noble deed. To be sure, he can bring in a proposition for the better protection of property in the District of Columbia, but he makes no allusion whatever, to the rights of black men. This proposition in relation to the rights of property, is regarded by his adherents as a noble act; as a timely measure; as indicating great courage and heroism. Nor do I care to deny it. But what is the inference? If it be a noble act, a courageous act, to move in the Capitol of the nation, in the Senate of the United States, a bill to protect property from the assaults of a brutal and ferocious mob,—if that be bold, of course it would be no less daring and fanatical to move in that District, that the rights of man be protected.

I do not propose to make a lengthy speech, but I would like to say a few words about how these things look to others.

> "O wad some power the giftie gie us
> To see oursels as others see us."

I would like to hold up to you a picture; not drawn by an American pen or pencil, but by a foreigner. I want to show you how you look abroad in the delectable business of kidnapping and slave driving.

Sometimes since—I think it was in the December number of "Punch,"—I saw an excellent pictorial description of America.—

What think you it was? It was entitled, "Brother Jonathan." It was a long, lean, gaunt, shriveled looking creature, stretched out on two chairs, and his legs resting on the prostrate bust of Washington; projecting from behind was a cat-o'-nine tails knotted at the ends; around his person he wore a belt in which were stuck those truly American implements, a bowie knife, dirk, and revolving pistol; behind him was a whipping post, with a naked woman tied to it, and a strong-armed American citizen in the act of scourging her livid flesh with a cowskin. At his feet was another group;—a sale going on, of human cattle, and around the auctioneer's table were gathered the respectability,—the religion represented in the person of the clergy,—of America, buying them for export to the goodly city of New Orleans. Little further on there was a scene of branding,—a small group of slaves tied hand and foot, while their patriotic and philanthropic masters were burning their name into their quivering flesh. Further on, there was a drove of slaves, bound for New Orleans. Above these and several other scenes illustrative of the character of our institutions, waved the star spangled banner. Still further back in the distance was the picture of the achievements of our gallant army in Mexico, shooting, stabbing, hanging; destroying property, and massacring the innocent with the innocent, not with the guilty, and over all this was a picture of the Devil himself, looking down with Satanic satisfaction on passing events.

Here I conceive to be a true picture of America, and I hesitate not to say that this description falls far short of the real facts, and of the aspect we bear to the world around us.

Sir, although we have heard conflicting views uttered here today, of hopeful and desponding aspects, (if, indeed, we have any desponding aspects brought to us,) still, I think much more may be said in behalf of the hopeful aspects. The signs of the times have been already alluded to; we have very properly gone beyond the limits of the United States.

I see some of the audience are going out, which makes me think I have spoken long enough; some plants thrive better by being cut off, and perhaps my speech may as well be cut off here; not because there is not more to be said, but because your energies have been taxed quite enough already. Since, then, you wish me to proceed, and, as Henry Clay says, "I am always subject to the will of the people," there may yet be room for something of a speech.

As I was proceeding to remark concerning the hopeful aspects of the times, I wish to bring with more distinctness before your minds, the news which comes from abroad—the action of the Provisional Government of France. We have been accustomed, in this country, to hear much talk about "Christian America, and Infidel France." I want to say in behalf of France, that I go for that infidelity—no matter how heinous it may be in the estimation of the American people—which strikes the chains from the limbs of our brethren; and against that Christianity which puts them on,—for that infidelity, which, in the person of Cremieux, one of the members of the Provisional Government of France, speaks to the black and mulatto men, that come to congratulate them, and express their sentiments upon the immediate emancipation of their brethren in the French islands. I sympathize with that infidelity that speaks to them in language like this: friends! brothers! men! In France, the Negro is a man, while you who are throwing up your caps, and waving your banners, and making beautiful speeches in behalf of liberty, deny us our humanity, and traffic in our flesh.

Sir, I would like to bring more vividly to before this audience, the wrongs of my downtrodden countrymen. I have no disposition to look at this matter in any sentimental light, but to bring before you stern facts, and keep forever before the American people the damning and disgraceful fact, that three millions of people are in chains today—that while we are here speaking in their behalf, saying noble words and doing noble deeds, they are under the yoke, smarting beneath the lash, sundered from each other, trafficked in and brutally treated; and that the American nation, to keep them in their present condition, stands ready with its ten thousand bayonets, to plunge them into their hearts. If they attempt to strike for their freedom, I want every man north of Mason and Dixon's line, whenever they attend an anti-slavery meeting, to remember that it is the Northern area that does this—that you are not only guilty of withholding your influence, but that you are the positive enemies of the slave, the positive holders of the slave, and that in your right arm rests the physical power that keeps him under the yoke.

I want you to feel that I am addressing slaveholders; speaking to men who have entered into a solemn league and covenant with the slaveholders of the country, that in any emergency, if at any time the spirit of freedom finds a lodgment in the bosom of the American slave, and they shall be moved to throw up barricades against their tyrants, as the French did in the streets of Paris, that you, every man of you that swears to support the Constitution, is sworn to pour leaden death into their hearts. I am speaking to slaveholders, and if I speak plainly, set it not down to impudence, but to opposition to Slavery. For God's sake, let a man speak when he cannot do anything else; when fetters are on his limbs, let him have this small right of making his wrongs known; at least, let it be done in New York. I am glad to see there is a disposition to let it be done here—to allow him to tell what is in him, with regard to his own personal wrongs at any rate.

Sir, I have been frequently denounced because I have dared to speak against the American nation, against the Church—the Northern churches especially, charging them with being the slaveholders of the country. I desire to say here, as elsewhere, that I am not at all ambitious of the ill opinions of my countrymen, nor do I desire their hatred; but I must say, as I have said, that I want no man's friendship, no matter how high he may stand in Church or State, I want no man's sympathies or approbation who is not ready to strike the chains from the limbs of my brethren. I do not ask the esteem and friendship of any minister or any man, no matter how high his standing, nor do I wish to shake any man's hand, who stands indifferent to the wrongs of my brethren. Some have boasted that when Fred Douglass has been at their houses, he has been treated kindly, but as soon as he got into their pulpits he began to abuse them—that as soon as the advantage is given him, he takes it to stab those who befriend him. Friends, I wish to stab no man, but if you stand on the side of the slaveholder, and cry out "the Union as it is," "the Constitution as it is," "the Church as it is," you may expect that the heart that throbs beneath this bosom, will give utterance against you. I am bound to speak, and, whenever there is an opportunity to do so, I will speak against Slavery.

I meant to have said a word about Colonization, as I observed there was a very dark-looking individual here, (Gov. Pinney, of Liberia,) for whose special benefit I wished to say something on that subject. But as I do not see him here now, there is no necessity to discuss this subject for his benefit. When he was pointed out to me, I thought it remarkable, that so dark a man should be in favor of colonization; but there are some simple-minded men even among colored people. I will just say, however, that we have had some advice given us lately, from very high authority. I allude to Henry Clay, who in his last speech before the Colonization Society, at Washington, advised the free colored people of the United States that they had better go to Africa.

He says he does not wish to coerce us, but thinks we had better go! What right has he to tell us to go? We have as much right to stay here as he has. I don't care if you did throw up your caps for him when he came to this city—I don't care if he did give you "his heart on the outside of the city Hall and his hand on the inside;" I have as much right to stay here as he has! And I want to say to our white friends, that we, colored folks, have had the subject under consideration, and have decided to stay! want to say to any colonization friends here, that they may give their minds no further uneasiness on our account, for our minds are made up. I think this is about the best argument on that subject.

Now there is one thing more about us colored folks; it is this, that under all these most adverse circumstances, we live and move and have our being, and that too in peace, and are almost persuaded that there is a providence in our staying here. I do not know but the United States would rot in its tyranny, if there were not some Negroes in this land— some to clink their chains in the care of listening humanity, and from whose prostrate forms the lessons of liberty can be taught to the whites.

It is through us now that you are learning that your own rights are stricken down.—At this time it is the Abolitionist that holds up the lamp that shows the political parties of the North their fetters and chains. A little while ago, and the Northern men were bound in the strange fanatic delusion, that they had something to do with making of Presidents of the United States: that is about given up now. No one now of common sense, or common reading, imagines for a moment that New York has anything to do with deciding who the President shall be. They are allowed to vote, but what is the amount of this privi- lege? It is to vote for the slaveholder, or whom the slaveholders select.

No men that are now accounted sane, think of any other than of a slaveholder or assassin, or both, who shall hold the destinies of the nation,—and the reason is because the people are convinced that they belong—as they used to say to the colored boys of the South, to the party. They used sometimes to ask me, "boy who do you belong to?" and I used to answer "to Captain Thomas Auld, of St. Michaels, a class- leader in the Methodist Episcopal church;" and now I would ask, "who do you belong to?" I will tell you. You belong to the Democratic Party, to the Whig Party, and these parties belong to the slaveholder, and the slaveholder rules the country. As the boy said about ruling England: "I rule mamma, and mamma rules papa, and papa rules the people, and the people rule England." To be sure you have the right to vote, which is like what I heard once of a certain boy, who said he was going to live with his uncle Robert, and when I go there, said he, I am going to do just as I please—if uncle Robert will let me!

The Northern people are going to do just as they please if the slave- holders will let them. The little bit of opposition that has manifested itself in that little protuberance on American politics—the Wilmot proviso—which our friend Gay has fully described as a tempest in a teapot, has now quite flattened down. The Whigs, who said we will stand by it at all hazards, have fairly backed out; they did so last fall; they got afraid of the Union. In Ohio I heard men striking their fists together, saying they would stand by it at all hazards; and after a little while, the Ohio State Legislature come to the conclusion, after having carefully considered the matter, that "to press the question of no more slave territory must be disastrous to our American Union."—New York came out expressly in favor of the Proviso and it has since seen that the Union will be periled by adherence to that principle. And all over the North there is this fainting away before that power which was before undefined, as has been so eloquently touched upon by my friend Phillips; for while men hold up their hands in favor of the Union and the Constitution, there is a moral conflict in their hearts, for, as was so beautifully expressed by Mr. Parker, of Boston, men cannot fight Slavery under the Constitution; the Constitution soils the amour about them; we cannot strike Slavery while we have it on us: there is no other way to throw it off.

I have no prepared speech, and I will not weary you any longer. I have sometimes thought since the late occurrences in France, that there may be an under current in men's hearts here as there was in Paris; Louis Philippe thought himself perfectly secure surrounded by his 300,000 soldiers, who, with fixed bayonets, were ready to support him in the suppression of the riots; but the troops were found to fraternize with the people; the soldier joined the civilian to assert and defend his rights. So I believe here, after all we have said against the American people, there is yet an under current pervading the mass of the people in this country, uniting Democrat and Whig, and men of no party, taking hold in quarters we know not of, which shall one day rise up in one glorious Fraternity for Freedom, uniting into one mighty phalanx of freemen to bring down the haughty citadel of Slavery with all its bloody towers and turrets.

> "There's a good time coming boys,
> A good time coming,
> Wait a little longer.
> We may not live to see the day,
> But earth shall glisten in the ray
> Of the good time coming;
> Cannon balls may aid the truth,
> But thought's a weapon stronger,
> We'll win our battle by its aid,
> Wait a little longer."

What to the Slave is the 4th of July?
(1852)

When asked to speak at the city of Rochester's annual Independence Day cel-ebration, Douglass chose not to deliver a patriotic address, but rather a scathing rebuke of the hypocrisy inherent in asking a former slave to present a speech on such an occasion. Delivered on July 5, 1852, this passionate, biting oratory would go on to become one of Douglass's most well-known and influential speeches.

Mr. President, Friends, and Fellow Citizens.

He who could address this audience without a quailing sensation, has stronger nerves than I have. I do not remember ever to have appeared as a speaker before any assembly more shrinkingly, nor with greater distrust of my ability, than I do this day. A feeling has crept over me quite unfavorable to the exercise of my limited powers of speech. The task before me is one which requires much previous thought and study for its proper performance. I know that apologies of this sort are generally considered flat and unmeaning. I trust, however, that mine will not be so considered. Should I seem at ease, my appearance would much misrepresent me. The little experience I have had in addressing public meetings, in country schoolhouses, avails me nothing on the present occasion.

The papers and placards say that I am to deliver a Fourth of July Oration. This certainly sounds large, and out of the common way, for me. It is true that I have often had the privilege to speak in this beautiful Hall, and to address many who now honor me with their presence. But neither their familiar faces, nor the perfect gage I think I have of Corinthian Hall seems to free me from embarrassment.

The fact is, ladies and gentlemen, the distance between this platform and the slave plantation, from which I escaped, is considerable—and the difficulties to be overcome in getting from the latter to the former are by no means slight. That I am here today is, to me, a matter of astonishment as well as of gratitude. You will not, therefore, be surprised, if in what I have to say I evince no elaborate preparation, nor grace my speech with any high sounding exordium. With little experience and with less learning, I have been able to throw my thoughts hastily and imperfectly together; and trusting to your patient and generous indulgence I will proceed to lay them before you.

This, for the purpose of this celebration, is the Fourth of July. It is the birthday of your National Independence, and of your political freedom. This, to you, is what the Passover was to the emancipated people of God. It carries your minds back to the day, and to the act of your great deliverance; and to the signs, and to the wonders, associated with that act, and that day. This celebration also marks the beginning of another year of your national life; and reminds you that the Republic of America is now 76 years old. I am glad, fellow-citizens, that your nation is so young. Seventy-six years, though a good old age for a man, is but a mere speck in the life of a nation. Three score years and ten is the allotted time for individual men; but nations number their years by thousands. According to this fact, you are, even now, only in the beginning of your national career, still lingering in the period of child-hood. I repeat, I am glad this is so. There is hope in the thought, and hope is much needed, under the dark clouds which lower above the horizon. The eye of the reformer is met with angry flashes, portending disastrous times; but his heart may well beat lighter at the thought that America is young, and that she is still in the impressible stage of her existence. May he not hope that high lessons of wisdom, of justice and of truth, will yet give direction to her destiny? Were the nation older, the patriot's heart might be sadder, and the reformer's brow heavier. Its future might be shrouded in gloom, and the hope of its prophets go out in sorrow. There is consolation in the thought that America is young. Great streams are not easily turned from channels, worn deep in the course of ages. They may sometimes rise in quiet and stately majesty, and inundate the land, refreshing and fertilizing the earth with their mysterious properties. They may also rise in wrath and fury, and bear away, on their angry waves, the accumulated wealth of years of toil and hardship. They, however, gradually flow back to the same old channel, and flow on as serenely as ever. But, while the river may not be turned aside, it may dry up, and leave nothing behind but the withered branch, and the unsightly rock, to howl in the abyss-sweeping wind, the sad tale of departed glory. As with rivers so with nations.

Fellow-citizens, I shall not presume to dwell at length on the associations that cluster about this day. The simple story of it is, that, 76 years ago, the people of this country were British subjects. The style and title of your "sovereign people" (in which you now glory) was not then born. You were under the British Crown. Your fathers esteemed the English Government as the home government; and England as the fatherland. This home government, you know, although a considerable distance from your home, did, in the exercise of its parental prerogatives, impose upon its colonial children, such restraints, burdens and limitations, as, in its mature judgment, it deemed wise, right and proper.

But your fathers, who had not adopted the fashionable idea of this day, of the infallibility of government, and the absolute character of its acts, presumed to differ from the home government in respect to the wisdom and the justice of some of those burdens and restraints. They went so far in their excitement as to pronounce the measures of government unjust, unreasonable, and oppressive, and altogether such as ought not to be quietly submitted to. I scarcely need say, fellow-citizens, that my opinion of those measures fully accords with that of your fathers. Such a declaration of agreement on my part would not be worth much to anybody. It would certainly prove nothing as to what part I might have taken had I lived during the great controversy of 1776. To say now that America was right, and England wrong, is exceedingly easy. Everybody can say it; the dastard, not less than the noble brave, can flippantly descant on the tyranny of England towards the American Colonies. It is fashionable to do so; but there was a time when, to pronounce against England, and in favor of the cause of the colonies, tried men's souls. They who did so were accounted in their day plotters of mischief, agitators and rebels, dangerous men. To side with the right against the wrong, with the weak against the strong, and with the oppressed against the oppressor! here lies the merit, and the one which, of all others, seems unfashionable in our day. The cause of liberty may be stabbed by the men who glory in the deeds of your fathers. But, to proceed.

Feeling themselves harshly and unjustly treated, by the home government, your fathers, like men of honesty, and men of spirit, earnestly sought redress. They petitioned and remonstrated; they did so in a decorous, respectful, and loyal manner. Their conduct was wholly unexceptionable. This, however, did not answer the purpose. They saw themselves treated with sovereign indifference, coldness and scorn. Yet they persevered. They were not the men to look back.

As the sheet anchor takes a firmer hold, when the ship is tossed by the storm, so did the cause of your fathers grow stronger as it breasted the chilling blasts of kingly displeasure. The greatest and best of British statesmen admitted its justice, and the loftiest eloquence of the British Senate came to its support. But, with that blindness which seems to be the unvarying characteristic of tyrants, since Pharaoh and his hosts were drowned in the Red Sea, the British Government persisted in the exactions complained of.

The madness of this course, we believe, is admitted now, even by England; but we fear the lesson is wholly lost on our present rulers.

Oppression makes a wise man mad. Your fathers were wise men, and if they did not go mad, they became restive under this treatment. They felt themselves the victims of grievous wrongs, wholly incurable in their colonial capacity. With brave men there is always a remedy for oppression. Just here, the idea of a total separation of the colonies from the crown was born! It was a startling idea, much more so than we, at this distance of time, regard it. The timid and the prudent (as has been intimated) of that day were, of course, shocked and alarmed by it.

Such people lived then, had lived before, and will, probably, ever have a place on this planet; and their course, in respect to any great change (no matter how great the good to be attained, or the wrong to be redressed by it), may be calculated with as much precision as can be the course of the stars. They hate all changes, but silver, gold and copper change! Of this sort of change they are always strongly in favor.

These people were called Tories in the days of your fathers; and the appellation, probably, conveyed the same idea that is meant by a more modern, though a somewhat less euphonious term, which we often find in our papers, applied to some of our old politicians.

Their opposition to the then dangerous thought was earnest and powerful; but, amid all their terror and affrighted vociferations against it, the alarming and revolutionary idea moved on, and the country with it.

On the 2nd of July, 1776, the old Continental Congress, to the dismay of the lovers of ease, and the worshipers of property, clothed that dreadful idea with all the authority of national sanction. They did so in the form of a resolution; and as we seldom hit upon resolutions, drawn up in our day, whose transparency is at all equal to this, it may refresh your minds and help my story if I read it.

> "Resolved, That these united colonies are, and of right, ought to be free and Independent States; that they are absolved from all allegiance to the British Crown; and that all political connection between them and the State of Great Britain is, and ought to be, dissolved."

Citizens, your fathers made good that resolution. They succeeded; and to day you reap the fruits of their success. The freedom gained is yours; and you, therefore, may properly celebrate this anniversary. The 4th of July is the first great fact in your nation's history—the very ringbolt in the chain of your yet undeveloped destiny.

Pride and patriotism, not less than gratitude, prompt you to celebrate and to hold it in perpetual remembrance. I have said that the

Declaration of Independence is the ringbolt to the chain of your nation's destiny; so, indeed, I regard it. The principles contained in that instrument are saving principles. Stand by those principles, be true to them on all occasions, in all places, against all foes, and at whatever cost.

From the round top of your ship of state, dark and threatening clouds may be seen. Heavy billows, like mountains in the distance, disclose to the leeward huge forms of flinty rocks! That bolt drawn, that chain broken, and all is lost. Cling to this day—cling to it, and to its principles, with the grasp of a storm-tossed mariner to a spar at midnight.

The coming into being of a nation, in any circumstances, is an interesting event. But, besides general considerations, there were peculiar circumstances which make the advent of this republic an event of special attractiveness. The whole scene, as I look back to it, was simple, dignified and sublime. The population of the country, at the time, stood at the insignificant number of three millions. The country was poor in the munitions of war. The population was weak and scattered, and the country a wilderness unsubdued. There were then no means of concert and combination, such as exist now. Neither steam nor lightning had then been reduced to order and discipline. From the Potomac to the Delaware was a journey of many days. Under these, and innumerable other disadvantages, your fathers declared for liberty and independence and triumphed.

Fellow Citizens, I am not wanting in respect for the fathers of this republic. The signers of the Declaration of Independence were brave men. They were great men, too—great enough to give frame to a great age. It does not often happen to a nation to raise, at one time, such a number of truly great men. The point from which I am compelled to view them is not, certainly, the most favorable; and yet I cannot contemplate their great deeds with less than admiration. They were statesmen, patriots and heroes, and for the good they did, and the principles they contended for, I will unite with you to honor their memory.

They loved their country better than their own private interests; and, though this is not the highest form of human excellence, all will concede that it is a rare virtue, and that when it is exhibited it ought to command respect. He who will, intelligently, lay down his life for his country is a man whom it is not in human nature to despise. Your fathers staked their lives, their fortunes, and their sacred honor, on the cause of their country. In their admiration of liberty, they lost sight of all other interests.

They were peace men; but they preferred revolution to peaceful submission to bondage. They were quiet men; but they did not shrink from agitating against oppression. They showed forbearance; but that they knew its limits. They believed in order; but not in the order of tyranny. With them, nothing was "settled" that was not right. With them, justice, liberty and humanity were "final"; not slavery and oppression. You may well cherish the memory of such men. They were great in their day and generation. Their solid manhood stands out the more as we contrast it with these degenerate times.

How circumspect, exact and proportionate were all their movements! How unlike the politicians of an hour! Their statesmanship looked beyond the passing moment, and stretched away in strength into the distant future. They seized upon eternal principles, and set a glorious example in their defense. Mark them! Fully appreciating the hardships to be encountered, firmly believing in the right of their cause, honorably inviting the scrutiny of an on looking world, reverently appealing to heaven to attest their sincerity, soundly comprehending the solemn responsibility they were about to assume, wisely measuring the terrible odds against them, your fathers, the fathers of this republic, did, most deliberately, under the inspiration of a glorious patriotism, and with a sublime faith in the great principles of justice and freedom, lay deep, the corner-stone of the national super-structure, which has risen and still rises in grandeur around you.

Of this fundamental work, this day is the anniversary. Our eyes are met with demonstrations of joyous enthusiasm. Banners and pennants wave exultingly on the breeze. The din of business, too, is hushed. Even mammon seems to have quitted his grasp on this day. The ear-piercing fife and the stirring drum unite their accents with the ascending peal of a thousand church bells. Prayers are made, hymns are sung, and sermons are preached in honor of this day; while the quick martial tramp of a great and multitudinous nation, echoed back by all the hills, valleys and mountains of a vast continent, bespeak the occasion one of thrilling and universal interest—a nation's jubilee.

Friends and citizens, I need not enter further into the causes which led to this anniversary. Many of you understand them better than I do. You could instruct me in regard to them. That is a branch of knowledge in which you feel, perhaps, a much deeper interest than your speaker. The causes which led to the separation of the colonies from the British crown have never lacked for a tongue. They have all been taught in your common schools, narrated at your firesides, unfolded from your pulpits, and thundered from your legislative halls, and are as familiar to you as household words. They form the staple of your national poetry and eloquence.

I remember, also, that, as a people, Americans are remarkably familiar with all facts which make in their own favor. This is esteemed by some as a national trait—perhaps a national weakness. It is a fact, that whatever makes for the wealth or for the reputation of Americans and

can be had cheap! will be found by Americans. I shall not be charged
with slandering Americans if I say I think the American side of any
question may be safely left in American hands.

I leave, therefore, the great deeds of your fathers to other gentlemen
whose claim to have been regularly descended will be less likely to be
disputed than mine!

My business, if I have any here today, is with the present. The accepted time with God and His cause is the ever living now.

> Trust no future, however pleasant,
> Let the dead past bury its dead;
> Act, act in the living present,
> Heart within, and God overhead.

We have to do with the past only as we can make it useful to the
present and to the future. To all inspiring motives, to noble deeds
which can be gained from the past, we are welcome. But now is the
time, the important time. Your fathers have lived, died, and have done
their work, and have done much of it well. You live and must die, and
you must do your work. You have no right to enjoy a child's share in
the labor of your fathers, unless your children are to be blest by your
labors. You have no right to wear out and waste the hard-earned fame
of your fathers to cover your indolence. Sydney Smith tells us that men
seldom eulogize the wisdom and virtues of their fathers, but to excuse
some folly or wickedness of their own. This truth is not a doubtful one.
There are illustrations of it near and remote, ancient and modern. It was
fashionable, hundreds of years ago, for the children of Jacob to boast,
we have "Abraham to our father," when they had long lost Abraham's
faith and spirit. That people contented themselves under the shadow
of Abraham's great name, while they repudiated the deeds which made
his name great. Need I remind you that a similar thing is being done all
over this country today? Need I tell you that the Jews are not the only
people who built the tombs of the prophets, and garnished the sepul-
chers of the righteous? Washington could not die till he had broken the
chains of his slaves. Yet his monument is built up by the price of human
blood, and the traders in the bodies and souls of men shout—"We have
Washington as our father."

> Alas! that it should be so; yet it is.
> The evil, that men do, lives after them,
> The good is oft interred with their bones.

Fellow-citizens, pardon me, allow me to ask, why am I called upon to
speak here today? What have I, or those I represent, to do with your
national independence? Are the great principles of political freedom

and of natural justice, embodied in that Declaration of Independence, extended to us? and am I, therefore, called upon to bring our humble offering to the national altar, and to confess the benefits and express devout gratitude for the blessings resulting from your independence to us?

Would to God, both for your sakes and ours, that an affirmative answer could be truthfully returned to these questions! Then would my task be light, and my burden easy and delightful. For who is there so cold, that a nation's sympathy could not warm him? Who so obdurate and dead to the claims of gratitude, that would not thankfully acknowledge such priceless benefits? Who so stolid and selfish, that would not give his voice to swell the hallelujahs of a nation's jubilee, when the chains of servitude had been torn from his limbs? I am not that man. In a case like that, the dumb might eloquently speak, and the "lame man leap as an hart."

But such is not the state of the case. I say it with a sad sense of the disparity between us. I am not included within the pale of this glorious anniversary! Your high independence only reveals the immeasurable distance between us. The blessings in which you, this day, rejoice, are not enjoyed in common. The rich inheritance of justice, liberty, prosperity and independence, bequeathed by your fathers, is shared by you, not by me. The sunlight that brought light and healing to you, has brought stripes and death to me. This Fourth July is yours, not mine. You may rejoice, I must mourn. To drag a man in fetters into the grand illuminated temple of liberty, and call upon him to join you in joyous anthems, were inhuman mockery and sacrilegious irony. Do you mean, citizens, to mock me, by asking me to speak today? If so, there is a parallel to your conduct. And let me warn you that it is dangerous to copy the example of a nation whose crimes, towering up to heaven, were thrown down by the breath of the Almighty, burying that nation in irrevocable ruin! I can today take up the plaintive lament of a peeled and woe-smitten people!

"By the rivers of Babylon, there we sat down. Yea! we wept when we remembered Zion. We hanged our harps upon the willows in the midst thereof. For there, they that carried us away captive, required of us a song; and they who wasted us required of us mirth, saying, Sing us one of the songs of Zion. How can we sing the Lord's song in a strange land? If I forget thee, O Jerusalem, let my right hand forget her cunning. If I do not remember thee, let my tongue cleave to the roof of my mouth."

Fellow-citizens, above your national, tumultuous joy, I hear the mournful wail of millions! whose chains, heavy and grievous yesterday, are, today, rendered more intolerable by the jubilee shouts that reach them. If I do forget, if I do not faithfully remember those bleeding children of sorrow this day, "may my right hand forget her cunning, and may my tongue cleave to the roof of my mouth!" To forget them, to pass lightly over their wrongs, and to chime in with the popular theme, would be treason most scandalous and shocking, and would make me a reproach before God and the world. My subject, then, fellow-citizens, is American slavery. I shall see this day and its popular characteristics from the slave's point of view. Standing there identified with the American bondman, making his wrongs mine, I do not hesitate to declare, with all my soul, that the character and conduct of this nation never looked blacker to me than on this 4th of July! Whether we turn to the declarations of the past, or to the professions of the present, the conduct of the nation seems equally hideous and revolting. America is false to the past, false to the present, and solemnly binds herself to be false to the future. Standing with God and the crushed and bleeding slave on this occasion, I will, in the name of humanity which is outraged, in the name of liberty which is fettered, in the name of the constitution and the Bible which are disregarded and trampled upon, dare to call in question and to denounce, with all the emphasis I can command, everything that serves to perpetuate slavery—the great sin and shame of America! "I will not equivocate; I will not excuse"; I will use the severest language I can command; and yet not one word shall escape me that any man, whose judgment is not blinded by prejudice, or who is not at heart a slaveholder, shall not confess to be right and just.

But I fancy I hear some one of my audience say, "It is just in this circumstance that you and your brother abolitionists fail to make a favorable impression on the public mind. Would you argue more, and denounce less; would you persuade more, and rebuke less; your cause would be much more likely to succeed." But, I submit, where all is plain there is nothing to be argued. What point in the anti slavery creed would you have me argue? On what branch of the subject do the people of this country need light? Must I undertake to prove that the slave is a man? That point is conceded already. Nobody doubts it. The slaveholders themselves acknowledge it in the enactment of laws for their government. They acknowledge it when they punish disobedience on the part of the slave. There are seventy-two crimes in the State of Virginia which, if committed by a black man (no matter how ignorant he be), subject him to the punishment of death; while only two of the same crimes will subject a white man to the like punishment. What is this but the acknowledgment that the slave is a moral, intellectual, and responsible being? The manhood of the slave is conceded. It is admitted in the fact that Southern statute books are covered with enactments forbidding, under severe fines and penalties, the teaching of the slave to read or to write. When you can point to any such laws in reference to the beasts of the field, then I may consent to argue the manhood of the slave. When the dogs in your streets, when the fowls of the air, when the cattle on your hills, when the fish of the sea, and the reptiles that crawl, shall be unable to distinguish the slave from a brute, then will I argue with you that the slave is a man!

For the present, it is enough to affirm the equal manhood of the Negro race. Is it not astonishing that, while we are plowing, planting, and reaping, using all kinds of mechanical tools, erecting houses, constructing bridges, building ships, working in metals of brass, iron, copper, silver and gold; that, while we are reading, writing and ciphering, acting as clerks, merchants and secretaries, having among us lawyers, doctors, ministers, poets, authors, editors, orators and teachers; that, while we are engaged in all manner of enterprises common to other men, digging gold in California, capturing the whale in the Pacific, feeding sheep and cattle on the hill-side, living, moving, acting, thinking, planning, living in families as husbands, wives and children, and, above all, confessing and worshipping the Christian's God, and looking hopefully for life and immortality beyond the grave, we are called upon to prove that we are men!

Would you have me argue that man is entitled to liberty? that he is the rightful owner of his own body? You have already declared it. Must I argue the wrongfulness of slavery? Is that a question for Republicans? Is it to be settled by the rules of logic and argumentation, as a matter beset with great difficulty, involving a doubtful application of the principle of justice, hard to be understood? How should I look today, in the presence of Americans, dividing, and subdividing a discourse, to show that men have a natural right to freedom? speaking of it relatively and positively, negatively and affirmatively. To do so, would be to make myself ridiculous, and to offer an insult to your understanding.—There is not a man beneath the canopy of heaven that does not know that slavery is wrong for him.

What, am I to argue that it is wrong to make men brutes, to rob them of their liberty, to work them without wages, to keep them ignorant of their relations to their fellow men, to beat them with sticks, to flay their flesh with the lash, to load their limbs with irons, to hunt them with dogs, to sell them at auction, to sunder their families, to knock out their teeth, to burn their flesh, to starve them into obedience and submission to their masters? Must I argue that a system thus marked with blood, and stained with pollution, is wrong? No! I will not. I have better employment for my time and strength than such arguments would imply.

What, then, remains to be argued? Is it that slavery is not divine; that God did not establish it; that our doctors of divinity are mistaken?

There is blasphemy in the thought. That which is inhuman, cannot be divine! Who can reason on such a proposition? They that can, may; I cannot. The time for such argument is passed.

At a time like this, scorching irony, not convincing argument, is needed. O! had I the ability, and could reach the nation's ear, I would, today, pour out a fiery stream of biting ridicule, blasting reproach, withering sarcasm, and stern rebuke. For it is not light that is needed, but fire; it is not the gentle shower, but thunder. We need the storm, the whirlwind, and the earthquake. The feeling of the nation must be quickened; the conscience of the nation must be roused; the propriety of the nation must be startled; the hypocrisy of the nation must be exposed; and its crimes against God and man must be proclaimed and denounced.

What, to the American slave, is your 4th of July? I answer; a day that reveals to him, more than all other days in the year, the gross injustice and cruelty to which he is the constant victim. To him, your celebration is a sham; your boasted liberty, an unholy license; your national greatness, swelling vanity; your sounds of rejoicing are empty and heartless; your denunciation of tyrants, brass fronted impudence; your shouts of liberty and equality, hollow mockery; your prayers and hymns, your sermons and thanksgivings, with all your religious parade and solemnity, are, to Him, mere bombast, fraud, deception, impiety, and hypocrisy—a thin veil to cover up crimes which would disgrace a nation of savages. There is not a nation on the earth guilty of practices more shocking and bloody than are the people of the United States, at this very hour.

Go where you may, search where you will, roam through all the monarchies and despotisms of the Old World, travel through South America, search out every abuse, and when you have found the last, lay your facts by the side of the everyday practices of this nation, and you will say with me, that, for revolting barbarity and shameless hypocrisy, America reigns without a rival.

Take the American slave-trade, which we are told by the papers, is especially prosperous just now. Ex-Senator Benton tells us that the price of men was never higher than now. He mentions the fact to show that slavery is in no danger. This trade is one of the peculiarities of American institutions. It is carried on in all the large towns and cities in one-half of this confederacy; and millions are pocketed every year by dealers in this horrid traffic. In several states this trade is a chief source of wealth. It is called (in contradistinction to the foreign slave-trade) "the internal slave-trade." It is, probably, called so, too, in order to divert from it the horror with which the foreign slave-trade is contemplated. That trade has long since been denounced by this government as piracy. It has been denounced with burning words from the high places of the nation as an execrable traffic. To arrest it, to put an end to it, this nation keeps a squadron, at immense cost, on the coast of Africa. Everywhere, in this country, it is safe to speak of this foreign slave-trade as a most inhuman traffic, opposed alike to the Laws of God and of man. The duty to extirpate and destroy it, is admitted even by our doctors of divinity. In order to put an end to it, some of these last have consented that their colored brethren (nominally free) should leave this country, and establish themselves on the western coast of Africa! It is, however, a notable fact that, while so much execration is poured out by Americans upon all those engaged in the foreign slave-trade, the men engaged in the slave-trade between the states pass without condemnation, and their business is deemed honorable.

Behold the practical operation of this internal slave-trade, the American slave-trade, sustained by American politics and American religion. Here you will see men and women reared like swine for the market. You know what is a swine-drover? I will show you a man-drover. They inhabit all our Southern States. They perambulate the country, and crowd the highways of the nation, with droves of human stock. You will see one of these human flesh jobbers, armed with pistol, whip, and bowie-knife, driving a company of a hundred men, women, and children, from the Potomac to the slave market at New Orleans. These wretched people are to be sold singly, or in lots, to suit purchasers. They are food for the cotton-field and the deadly sugar-mill. Mark the sad procession, as it moves wearily along, and the inhuman wretch who drives them. Hear his savage yells and his blood-curdling oaths, as he hurries on his affrighted captives! There, see the old man with locks thinned and gray. Cast one glance, if you please, upon that young mother, whose shoulders are bare to the scorching sun, her briny tears falling on the brow of the babe in her arms. See, too, that girl of thirteen, weeping, yes! weeping, as she thinks of the mother from whom she has been torn! The drove moves tardily. Heat and sorrow have nearly consumed their strength; suddenly you hear a quick snap, like the discharge of a rifle; the fetters clank, and the chain rattles simultaneously; your ears are saluted with a scream, that seems to have torn its way to the centre of your soul. The crack you heard was the sound of the slave-whip; the scream you heard was from the woman you saw with the babe. Her speed had faltered under the weight of her child and her chains! that gash on her shoulder tells her to move on. Follow this drove to New Orleans. Attend the auction; see men examined like horses; see the forms of women rudely and brutally exposed to the shocking gaze of American slave-buyers. See this drove sold and separated forever; and never forget the deep, sad sobs that arose from that scattered multitude. Tell me, citizens, where, under the sun, you can witness a spectacle more fiendish and shocking. Yet this is but a glance at the American slave-trade, as it exists, at this moment, in the ruling part of the United States.

I was born amid such sights and scenes. To me the American slave-trade is a terrible reality. When a child, my soul was often pierced with a sense of its horrors. I lived on Philpot Street, Fell's Point, Baltimore, and have watched from the wharves the slave ships in the Basin, anchored from the shore, with their cargoes of human flesh, waiting for favorable winds to waft them down the Chesapeake. There was, at that time, a grand slave mart kept at the head of Pratt Street, by Austin Woldfolk. His agents were sent into every town and county in Maryland, announcing their arrival, through the papers, and on flaming "hand-bills," headed cash for Negroes. These men were generally well-dressed men, and very captivating in their manners; ever ready to drink, to treat, and to gamble. The fate of many a slave has depended upon the turn of a single card; and many a child has been snatched from the arms of its mother by bargains arranged in a state of brutal drunkenness.

The flesh-mongers gather up their victims by dozens, and drive them, chained, to the general depot at Baltimore. When a sufficient number has been collected here, a ship is chartered for the purpose of conveying the forlorn crew to Mobile, or to New Orleans. From the slave prison to the ship, they are usually driven in the darkness of night; for since the antislavery agitation, a certain caution is observed.

In the deep, still darkness of midnight, I have been often aroused by the dead, heavy footsteps, and the piteous cries of the chained gangs that passed our door. The anguish of my boyish heart was intense; and I was often consoled, when speaking to my mistress in the morning, to hear her say that the custom was very wicked; that she hated to hear the rattle of the chains and the heart-rending cries. I was glad to find one who sympathized with me in my horror.

Fellow-citizens, this murderous traffic is, today, in active operation in this boasted republic. In the solitude of my spirit I see clouds of dust raised on the highways of the South; I see the bleeding footsteps; I hear the doleful wail of fettered humanity on the way to the slave-markets, where the victims are to be sold like horses, sheep, and swine, knocked off to the highest bidder. There I see the tenderest ties ruthlessly broken, to gratify the lust, caprice and rapacity of the buyers and sellers of men. My soul sickens at the sight.

Is this the land your Fathers loved,
The freedom which they toiled to win?
Is this the earth whereon they moved?
Are these the graves they slumber in?

But a still more inhuman, disgraceful, and scandalous state of things remains to be presented. By an act of the American Congress, not yet two years old, slavery has been nationalized in its most horrible and revolting form. By that act, Mason and Dixon's line has been obliterated; New York has become as Virginia; and the power to hold, hunt, and sell men, women and children, as slaves, remains no longer a mere state institution, but is now an institution of the whole United States. The power is co-extensive with the Star-Spangled Banner, and American Christianity. Where these go, may also go the merciless slave-hunter. Where these are, man is not sacred. He is a bird for the sportsman's gun. By that most foul and fiendish of all human decrees, the liberty and person of every man are put in peril. Your broad republican domain is hunting ground for men. Not for thieves and robbers, enemies of society, merely, but for men guilty of no crime. Your lawmakers have commanded all good citizens to engage in this hellish sport. Your President, your Secretary of State, your lords, nobles, and ecclesiastics enforce, as a duty you owe to your free and glorious country, and to your God, that you do this accursed thing. Not fewer than forty Americans have, within the past two years, been hunted down and, without a moment's warning, hurried away in chains, and consigned to slavery and excruciating torture. Some of these have had wives and children, dependent on them for bread; but of this, no account was made. The right of the hunter to his prey stands superior to the right of marriage, and to all rights in this republic, the rights of God included! For black men there is neither law nor justice, humanity nor religion. The Fugitive Slave Law makes mercy to them a crime; and bribes the judge who tries them. An American judge gets ten dollars for every victim he consigns to slavery, and five, when he fails to do so. The oath of any two villains is sufficient, under this hell-black enactment, to send the most pious and exemplary black man into the remorseless jaws of slavery! His own testimony is nothing. He can bring no witnesses for himself. The minister of American justice is bound by the law to hear but one side; and that side is the side of the oppressor. Let this damning fact be perpetually told. Let it be thundered around the world that in tyrant-killing, king-hating, people-loving, democratic, Christian America the seats of justice are filled with judges who hold their offices under an open and palpable bribe, and are bound, in deciding the case of a man's liberty, to hear only his accusers!

In glaring violation of justice, in shameless disregard of the forms of administering law, in cunning arrangement to entrap the defenseless, and in diabolical intent this Fugitive Slave Law stands alone in the annals of tyrannical legislation. I doubt if there be another nation on the globe having the brass and the baseness to put such a law on the statute book. If any man in this assembly thinks differently from me in this matter, and feels able to disprove my statements, I will gladly confront him at any suitable time and place he may select.

I take this law to be one of the grossest infringements of Christian Liberty, and, if the churches and ministers of our country were not stupidly blind, or most wickedly indifferent, they, too, would so regard it.

At the very moment that they are thanking God for the enjoyment of civil and religious liberty, and for the right to worship God according to the dictates of their own consciences, they are utterly silent in respect to a law which robs religion of its chief significance and makes it utterly worthless to a world lying in wickedness. Did this law concern the "mint, anise, and cumin"—abridge the right to sing psalms, to partake of the sacrament, or to engage in any of the ceremonies of religion, it would be smitten by the thunder of a thousand pulpits. A general shout would go up from the church demanding repeal, repeal, instant repeal! And it would go hard with that politician who presumed to solicit the votes of the people without inscribing this motto on his banner. Further, if this demand were not complied with, another Scotland would be added to the history of religious liberty, and the stern old covenanters would be thrown into the shade. A John Knox would be seen at every church door and heard from every pulpit, and Fillmore would have no more quarter than was shown by Knox to the beautiful, but treacherous, Queen Mary of Scotland. The fact that the church of our country (with fractional exceptions) does not esteem "the Fugitive Slave Law" as a declaration of war against religious liberty, implies that that church regards religion simply as a form of worship, an empty ceremony, and not a vital principle, requiring active benevolence, justice, love, and good will towards man. It esteems sacrifice above mercy; psalm singing above right doing; solemn meetings above practical righteousness. A worship that can be conducted by persons who refuse to give shelter to the houseless, to give bread to the hungry, clothing to the naked, and who enjoin obedience to a law forbidding these acts of mercy is a curse, not a blessing to mankind. The Bible addresses all such persons as "scribes, Pharisees, hypocrites, who pay tithe of mint, anise, and cummin, and have omitted the weightier matters of the law, judgment, mercy, and faith."

But the church of this country is not only indifferent to the wrongs of the slave, it actually takes sides with the oppressors. It has made itself the bulwark of American slavery, and the shield of American slave-hunters. Many of its most eloquent Divines, who stand as the very lights of the church, have shamelessly given the sanction of religion and the Bible to the whole slave system. They have taught that man may, properly, be a slave; that the relation of master and slave is ordained of

God; that to send back an escaped bondman to his master is clearly the duty of all the followers of the Lord Jesus Christ; and this horrible blasphemy is palmed off upon the world for Christianity.

For my part, I would say, welcome infidelity! welcome atheism! welcome anything! in preference to the gospel, as preached by those Divines! They convert the very name of religion into an engine of tyranny and barbarous cruelty, and serve to confirm more infidels, in this age, than all the infidel writings of Thomas Paine, Voltaire, and Bolingbroke put together have done! These ministers make religion a cold and flinty-hearted thing, having neither principles of right action nor bowels of compassion. They strip the love of God of its beauty and leave the throne of religion a huge, horrible, repulsive form. It is a religion for oppressors, tyrants, man-stealers, and thugs. It is not that "pure and undefiled religion" which is from above, and which is "first pure, then peaceable, easy to be entreated, full of mercy and good fruits, without partiality, and without hypocrisy." But a religion which favors the rich against the poor; which exalts the proud above the humble; which divides mankind into two classes, tyrants and slaves; which says to the man in chains, stay there; and to the oppressor, oppress on; it is a religion which may be professed and enjoyed by all the robbers and enslavers of mankind; it makes God a respecter of persons, denies his fatherhood of the race, and tramples in the dust the great truth of the brotherhood of man. All this we affirm to be true of the popular church, and the popular worship of our land and nation—a religion, a church, and a worship which, on the authority of inspired wisdom, we pronounce to be an abomination in the sight of God. In the language of Isaiah, the American church might be well addressed, "Bring no more vain oblations; incense is an abomination unto me: the new moons and Sabbaths, the calling of assemblies, I cannot away with; it is iniquity, even the solemn meeting. Your new moons, and your appointed feasts my soul hateth. They are a trouble to me; I am weary to bear them; and when ye spread forth your hands I will hide mine eyes from you. Yea when ye make many prayers, I will not hear. Your hands are full of blood; cease to do evil, learn to do well; seek judgment; relieve the oppressed; judge for the fatherless; plead for the widow."

The American church is guilty, when viewed in connection with what it is doing to uphold slavery; but it is superlatively guilty when viewed in its connection with its ability to abolish slavery.

The sin of which it is guilty is one of omission as well as of commission. Albert Barnes but uttered what the common sense of every man at all observant of the actual state of the case will receive as truth, when he declared that "There is no power out of the church that could sustain slavery an hour, if it were not sustained in it."

Let the religious press, the pulpit, the Sunday School, the conference meeting, the great ecclesiastical, missionary, Bible and tract associations of the land array their immense powers against slavery, and slaveholding; and the whole system of crime and blood would be scattered to the winds, and that they do not do this involves them in the most awful responsibility of which the mind can conceive.

In prosecuting the anti-slavery enterprise, we have been asked to spare the church, to spare the ministry; but how, we ask, could such a thing be done? We are met on the threshold of our efforts for the redemption of the slave, by the church and ministry of the country, in battle arrayed against us; and we are compelled to fight or flee. From what quarter, I beg to know, has proceeded a fire so deadly upon our ranks, during the last two years, as from the Northern pulpit? As the champions of oppressors, the chosen men of American theology have appeared—men honored for their so-called piety, and their real learning. The Lords of Buffalo, the Springs of New York, the Lathrops of Auburn, the Coxes and Spencers of Brooklyn, the Gannets and Sharps of Boston, the Deweys of Washington, and other great religious lights of the land have, in utter denial of the authority of Him by whom they professed to be called to the ministry, deliberately taught us, against the example of the Hebrews, and against the remonstrance of the Apostles, that we ought to obey man's law before the law of God.

My spirit wearies of such blasphemy; and how such men can be supported, as the "standing types and representatives of Jesus Christ," is a mystery which I leave others to penetrate. In speaking of the American church, however, let it be distinctly understood that I mean the great mass of the religious organizations of our land. There are exceptions, and I thank God that there are. Noble men may be found, scattered all over these Northern States, of whom Henry Ward Beecher, of Brooklyn; Samuel J. May, of Syracuse; and my esteemed friend (Rev. R. R. Raymond) on the platform, are shining examples; and let me say further, that, upon these men lies the duty to inspire our ranks with high religious faith and zeal, and to cheer us on in the great mission of the slave's redemption from his chains.

One is struck with the difference between the attitude of the American church towards the anti-slavery movement, and that occupied by the churches in England towards a similar movement in that country. There, the church, true to its mission of ameliorating, elevating and improving the condition of mankind, came forward promptly, bound up the wounds of the West Indian slave, and re stored him to his liberty. There, the question of emancipation was a high religious question. It was demanded in the name of humanity, and according to the law of the living God. The Sharps, the Clarksons, the Wilberforces, the Buxtons, the Burchells, and the Knibbs were alike famous for their piety and for their philanthropy. The anti-slavery movement there was not an anti-church movement, for the reason that the church took its full share in prosecuting that movement: and the anti-slavery movement in this country will cease to be an anti-church movement, when the church of this country shall assume a favorable instead of a hostile position towards that movement.

Americans! your republican politics, not less than your republican religion, are flagrantly inconsistent. You boast of your love of liberty, your superior civilization, and your pure Christianity, while the whole political power of the nation (as embodied in the two great political parties) is solemnly pledged to support and perpetuate the enslavement of three millions of your countrymen. You hurl your anathemas at the crowned headed tyrants of Russia and Austria and pride yourselves on your Democratic institutions, while you yourselves consent to be the mere tools and bodyguards of the tyrants of Virginia and Carolina. You invite to your shores fugitives of oppression from abroad, honor them with banquets, greet them with ovations, cheer them, toast them, salute them, protect them, and pour out your money to them like water; but the fugitives from oppression in your own land you advertise, hunt, arrest, shoot, and kill. You glory in your refinement and your universal education; yet you maintain a system as barbarous and dreadful as ever stained the character of a nation—a system begun in avarice, supported in pride, and perpetuated in cruelty. You shed tears over fallen Hungary, and make the sad story of her wrongs the theme of your poets, statesmen, and orators, till your gallant sons are ready to fly to arms to vindicate her cause against the oppressor; but, in regard to the ten thousand wrongs of the American slave, you would enforce the strictest silence, and would hail him as an enemy of the nation who dares to make those wrongs the subject of public discourse! You are all on fire at the mention of liberty for France or for Ireland; but are as cold as an iceberg at the thought of liberty for the enslaved of America. You discourse eloquently on the dignity of labor; yet, you sustain a system which, in its very essence, casts a stigma upon labor. You can bare your bosom to the storm of British artillery to throw off a three-penny tax on tea; and yet wring the last hard earned farthing from the grasp of the black laborers of your country. You profess to believe "that, of one blood, God made all nations of men to dwell on the face of all the earth," and hath commanded all men, everywhere, to love one another; yet you notoriously hate (and glory in your hatred) all men whose skins are not colored like your own. You declare before the world, and are understood by the world to declare that you "hold these truths to be self-evident, that all men are created equal; and are endowed by their

Creator with certain inalienable rights; and that among these are, life, liberty, and the pursuit of happiness; and yet, you hold securely, in a bondage which, according to your own Thomas Jefferson, "is worse than ages of that which your fathers rose in rebellion to oppose," a seventh part of the inhabitants of your country.

Fellow-citizens, I will not enlarge further on your national inconsistencies. The existence of slavery in this country brands your republicanism as a sham, your humanity as a base pretense, and your Christianity as a lie. It destroys your moral power abroad: it corrupts your politicians at home. It saps the foundation of religion; it makes your name a hissing and a byword to a mocking earth. It is the antagonistic force in your government, the only thing that seriously disturbs and endangers your Union. It fetters your progress; it is the enemy of improvement; the deadly foe of education; it fosters pride; it breeds insolence; it promotes vice; it shelters crime; it is a curse to the earth that supports it; and yet you cling to it as if it were the sheet anchor of all your hopes. Oh! be warned! be warned! a horrible reptile is coiled up in your nation's bosom; the venomous creature is nursing at the tender breast of your youthful republic; for the love of God, tear away, and fling from you the hideous monster, and let the weight of twenty millions crush and destroy it forever!

But it is answered in reply to all this, that precisely what I have now denounced is, in fact, guaranteed and sanctioned by the Constitution of the United States; that, the right to hold, and to hunt slaves is a part of that Constitution framed by the illustrious Fathers of this Republic.

★ ★ ★

Then, I dare to affirm, notwithstanding all I have said before, your fathers stooped, basely stooped,

> To palter with us in a double sense:
> And keep the word of promise to the ear,
> But break it to the heart.

And instead of being the honest men I have before declared them to be, they were the veriest impostors that ever practiced on mankind. This is the inevitable conclusion, and from it there is no escape; but I differ from those who charge this baseness on the framers of the Constitution of the United States. It is a slander upon their memory, at least, so I believe. There is not time now to argue the constitutional question at length; nor have I the ability to discuss it as it ought to be discussed. The subject has been handled with masterly power by Lysander Spooner, Esq. by William Goodell, by Samuel E. Sewall, Esq., and last, though not least, by Gerrit Smith, Esq. These gentlemen have, as I think, fully and clearly vindicated the Constitution from any design to support slavery for an hour.

Fellow-citizens! there is no matter in respect to which the people of the North have allowed themselves to be so ruinously imposed upon as that of the pro-slavery character of the Constitution. In that instrument I hold there is neither warrant, license, nor sanction of the hateful thing; but interpreted, as it ought to be interpreted, the Constitution is a glorious liberty document. Read its preamble, consider its purposes. Is slavery among them? Is it at the gate way? or is it in the temple? it is neither. While I do not intend to argue this question on the present occasion, let me ask, if it be not somewhat singular that, if the Constitution were intended to be, by its framers and adopters, a slaveholding instrument, why neither slavery, slaveholding, nor slave can anywhere be found in it. What would be thought of an instrument, drawn up, legally drawn up, for the purpose of entitling the city of Rochester to a tract of land, in which no mention of land was made? Now, there are certain rules of interpretation for the proper understanding of all legal instruments. These rules are well established. They are plain, common-sense rules, such as you and I, and all of us, can understand and apply, without having passed years in the study of law. I scout the idea that the question of the constitutionality, or unconstitutionality of slavery, is not a question for the people. I hold that every American citizen has a right to form an opinion of the constitution, and to propagate that opinion, and to use all honorable means to make his opinion the prevailing one. Without this right, the liberty of an American citizen would be as insecure as that of a Frenchman. Ex-Vice-President Dallas tells us that the constitution is an object to which no American mind can be too attentive, and no American heart too devoted. He further says, the Constitution, in its words, is plain and intelligible, and is meant for the home-bred, unsophisticated understandings of our fellow-citizens. Senator Berrien tells us that the Constitution is the fundamental law, that which controls all others. The charter of our liberties, which every citizen has a personal interest in understanding thoroughly. The testimony of Senator Breese, Lewis Cass, and many others that might be named, who are everywhere esteemed as sound lawyers, so regard the constitution. I take it, therefore, that it is not presumption in a private citizen to form an opinion of that instrument.

Now, take the Constitution according to its plain reading, and I defy the presentation of a single pro-slavery clause in it. On the other hand, it will be found to contain principles and purposes, entirely hostile to the existence of slavery.

I have detained my audience entirely too long already. At some future period I will gladly avail myself of an opportunity to give this subject a full and fair discussion.

Allow me to say, in conclusion, notwithstanding the dark picture I have this day presented, of the state of the nation, I do not despair of this country. There are forces in operation which must inevitably work the downfall of slavery.

"The arm of the Lord is not shortened," and the doom of slavery is certain. I, therefore, leave off where I began, with hope. While drawing encouragement from "the Declaration of Independence," the great principles it contains, and the genius of American Institutions, my spirit is also cheered by the obvious tendencies of the age. Nations do not now stand in the same relation to each other that they did ages ago. No nation can now shut itself up from the surrounding world and trot round in the same old path of its fathers without interference. The time was when such could be done. Long established customs of hurtful character could formerly fence themselves in, and do their evil work with social impunity. Knowledge was then confined and enjoyed by the privileged few, and the multitude walked on in mental darkness. But a change has now come over the affairs of mankind. Walled cities and empires have become unfashionable. The arm of commerce has borne away the gates of the strong city. Intelligence is penetrating the darkest corners of the globe. It makes its pathway over and under the sea, as well as on the earth. Wind, steam, and lightning are its chartered agents. Oceans no longer divide, but link nations together. From Boston to London is now a holiday excursion. Space is comparatively annihilated. Thoughts expressed on one side of the Atlantic are distinctly heard on the other.

The far off and almost fabulous Pacific rolls in grandeur at our feet. The Celestial Empire, the mystery of ages, is being solved. The fiat of the Almighty, "Let there be Light," has not yet spent its force. No abuse, no outrage whether in taste, sport or avarice, can now hide itself from the all-pervading light. The iron shoe, and crippled foot of China must be seen in contrast with nature. Africa must rise and put on her yet unwoven garment. "Ethiopia shall stretch out her hand unto God." In the fervent aspirations of William Lloyd Garrison, I say, and let every heart join in saying it:

> God speed the year of jubilee
> The wide world o'er!
> When from their galling chains set free,
> Th' oppress'd shall vilely bend the knee,
>
> And wear the yoke of tyranny
> Like brutes no more.

That year will come, and freedom's reign.
To man his plundered rights again
Restore.

God speed the day when human blood
Shall cease to flow!
In every clime be understood,
The claims of human brotherhood,
And each return for evil, good,
Not blow for blow.

That day will come all feuds to end,
And change into a faithful friend
Each foe.

A Plea for Free Speech in Boston
(1860)

In this address, Douglass responds to the breaking up of an anti-slavery meeting by a "mob of gentlemen" just a few days prior, describing the event as particularly instructive of the pro-slavery movement, as it was conducted by men who "pride themselves upon their respect for law and order." This speech was delivered at Music Hall in Boston, just 6 months before the outbreak of the Civil War, on December 4, 1860.

Boston is a great city—and Music Hall has a fame almost as extensive as that of Boston. Nowhere more than here have the principles of human freedom been expounded. But for the circumstances already mentioned, it would seem almost presumption for me to say anything here about those principles. And yet, even here, in Boston, the moral atmosphere is dark and heavy. The principles of human liberty, even if correctly apprehended, find but limited support in this hour of trial. The world moves slowly, and Boston is much like the world. We thought the principle of free speech was an accomplished fact. Here, if nowhere else, we thought the right of the people to assemble and to express their opinion was secure. Dr. Channing had defended the right, Mr. Garrison had practically asserted the right, and Theodore Parker had maintained it with steadiness and fidelity to the last.

But here we are today contending for what we thought was gained years ago. The mortifying and disgraceful fact stares us in the face, that though Faneuil Hall and Bunker Hill Monument stand, freedom of speech is struck down. No lengthy detail of facts is needed. They are already notorious; far more so than will be wished ten years hence.

The world knows that last Monday a meeting assembled to discuss the question: "How Shall Slavery Be Abolished?" The world also knows that that meeting was invaded, insulted, captured, by a mob of gentlemen, and thereafter broken up and dispersed by the order of the mayor, who refused to protect it, though called upon to do so. If this had been a mere outbreak of passion and prejudice among the baser

48

sort, maddened by rum and hounded on by some wily politician to serve some immediate purpose,—a mere exceptional affair,—it might be allowed to rest with what has already been said. But the leaders of the mob were gentlemen. They were men who pride themselves upon their respect for law and order.

These gentlemen brought their respect for the law with them and proclaimed it loudly while in the very act of breaking the law. Theirs was the law of slavery. The law of free speech and the law for the protection of public meetings they trampled under foot, while they greatly magnified the law of slavery.

The scene was an instructive one. Men seldom see such a blending of the gentleman with the rowdy, as was shown on that occasion. It proved that human nature is very much the same, whether in tarpaulin or broadcloth. Nevertheless, when gentlemen approach us in the character of lawless and abandoned loafers,—assuming for the moment their manners and tempers,—they have themselves to blame if they are estimated below their quality.

No right was deemed by the fathers of the Government more sacred than the right of speech. It was in their eyes, as in the eyes of all thoughtful men, the great moral renovator of society and government. Daniel Webster called it a homebred right, a fireside privilege. Liberty is meaningless where the right to utter one's thoughts and opinions has ceased to exist. That, of all rights, is the dread of tyrants. It is the right which they first of all strike down. They know its power. Thrones, dominions, principalities, and powers, founded in injustice and wrong, are sure to tremble, if men are allowed to reason of righteousness, temperance, and of a judgment to come in their presence. Slavery cannot tolerate free speech. Five years of its exercise would banish the auction block and break every chain in the South. They will have none of it there, for they have the power. But shall it be so here?

Even here in Boston, and among the friends of freedom, we hear two voices: one denouncing the mob that broke up our meeting on Monday as a base and cowardly outrage; and another, deprecating and regretting the holding of such a meeting, by such men, at such a time. We are told that the meeting was ill-timed, and the parties to it unwise.

Why, what is the matter with us? Are we going to palliate and excuse a palpable and flagrant outrage on the right of speech, by implying that only a particular description of persons should exercise that right? Are we, at such a time, when a great principle has been struck down, to quench the moral indignation which the deed excites, by casting reflections upon those on whose persons the outrage has been committed? After all the arguments for liberty to which Boston has listened for more than a quarter of a century, has she yet to learn that the time to assert a right is the time when the right itself is called in question, and that the men of all others to assert it are the men to whom the right has been denied?

It would be no vindication of the right of speech to prove that certain gentlemen of great distinction, eminent for their learning and ability, are allowed to freely express their opinions on all subjects—including the subject of slavery. Such a vindication would need, itself, to be vindicated. It would add insult to injury. Not even an old-fashioned abolition meeting could vindicate that right in Boston just now. There can be no right of speech where any man, however lifted up, or however humble, however young, or however old, is overawed by force, and compelled to suppress his honest sentiments.

Equally clear is the right to hear. To suppress free speech is a double wrong. It violates the rights of the hearer as well as those of the speaker. It is just as criminal to rob a man of his right to speak and hear as it would be to rob him of his money. I have no doubt that Boston will vindicate this right. But in order to do so, there must be no concessions to the enemy. When a man is allowed to speak because he is rich and powerful, it aggravates the crime of denying the right to the poor and humble.

The principle must rest upon its own proper basis. And until the right is accorded to the humblest as freely as to the most exalted citizen, the government of Boston is but an empty name, and its freedom a mockery. A man's right to speak does not depend upon where he was born or upon his color. The simple quality of manhood is the solid basis of the right—and there let it rest forever.

What the Black Man Wants
(1865)

In one of his most famous speeches, Frederick Douglas lays out his argument on why African Americans both desire and deserve not mere "generosity," but full equality and suffrage under the law. Delivered within days of Lincoln's assassination and the end of the civil war, this speech took place in early April of 1865 at the Annual Meeting of the Massachusetts Anti-Slavery Society in Boston.

I came here, as I come always to the meetings in New England, as a listener, and not as a speaker; and one of the reasons why I have not been more frequently to the meetings of this society, has been because of the disposition on the part of some of my friends to call me out upon the platform, even when they knew that there was some difference of opinion and of feeling between those who rightfully belong to this platform and myself; and for fear of being misconstrued, as desiring to interrupt or disturb the proceedings of these meetings, I have usually kept away, and have thus been deprived of that educating influence, which I am always free to confess is of the highest order, descending from this platform. I have felt, since I have lived out West[1], that in going there I parted from a great deal that was valuable; and I feel, every time I come to these meetings, that I have lost a great deal by making my home west of Boston, west of Massachusetts; for, if anywhere in the country there is to be found the highest sense of justice, or the truest demands for my race, I look for it in the East, I look for it here. The ablest discussions of the whole question of our rights occur here, and to be deprived of the privilege of listening to those discussions is a great deprivation.

I do not know, from what has been said, that there is any difference of opinion as to the duty of abolitionists, at the present moment. How can we get up any difference at this point, or any point, where we are so united, so agreed? I went especially, however, with that word of Mr.

---

1. Douglass means west of Boston, in Rochester, NY.

Phillips, which is the criticism of Gen. Banks and Gen. Banks' policy.[2] I hold that that policy is our chief danger at the present moment; that it practically enslaves the Negro, and makes the Proclamation[3] of 1863 a mockery and delusion. What is freedom? It is the right to choose one's own employment. Certainly it means that, if it means anything; and when any individual or combination of individuals undertakes to decide for any man when he shall work, where he shall work, at what he shall work, and for what he shall work, he or they practically reduce him to slavery. He is a slave. That I understand Gen. Banks to do—to determine for the so-called freedman, when, and where, and at what, and for how much he shall work, when he shall be punished, and by whom punished. It is absolute slavery. It defeats the beneficent intention of the Government, if it has beneficent intentions, in regards to the freedom of our people.

I have had but one idea for the last three years to present to the American people, and the phraseology in which I clothe it is the old abolition phraseology. I am for the "immediate, unconditional, and universal" enfranchisement of the black man, in every State in the Union. Without this, his liberty is a mockery; without this, you might as well almost retain the old name of slavery for his condition; for in fact, if he is not the slave of the individual master, he is the slave of society, and holds his liberty as a privilege, not as a right. He is at the mercy of the mob, and has no means of protecting himself.

It may be objected, however, that this pressing of the Negro's right to suffrage is premature. Let us have slavery abolished, it may be said, let us have labor organized, and then, in the natural course of events, the right of suffrage will be extended to the Negro. I do not agree with this. The constitution of the human mind is such, that if it once disregards the conviction forced upon it by a revelation of truth, it requires the exercise of a higher power to produce the same conviction afterwards. The American people are now in tears. The Shenandoah has run blood—the best blood of the North. All around Richmond, the blood of New England and of the North has been shed—of your sons, your brothers and your fathers. We all feel, in the existence of this Rebellion, that judgments terrible, wide-spread, far-reaching, overwhelming, are abroad in the land; and we feel, in view of these judgments, just now, a disposition to learn righteousness. This is the hour. Our streets are in

2. Gen. Banks instituted a labor policy in Louisiana that was discriminatory of blacks, claiming that it was to help prepare them to better handle freedom. Wendell Phillips countered by saying, "If there is anything patent in the whole history of our thirty years' struggle, it is that the Negro no more needs to be prepared for liberty than the white man."
3. The Emancipation Proclamation.

mourning, tears are falling at every fireside, and under the chastisement of this Rebellion we have almost come up to the point of conceding this great, this all-important right of suffrage. I fear that if we fail to do it now, if abolitionists fail to press it now, we may not see, for centuries to come, the same disposition that exists at this moment. Hence, I say, now is the time to press this right.

It may be asked, "Why do you want it? Some men have got along very well without it. Women have not this right." Shall we justify one wrong by another? This is the sufficient answer. Shall we at this moment justify the deprivation of the Negro of the right to vote, because some one else is deprived of that privilege? I hold that women, as well as men, have the right to vote, and my heart and voice go with the movement to extend suffrage to woman; but that question rests upon another basis than which our right rests. We may be asked, I say, why we want it. I will tell you why we want it. We want it because it is our right, first of all. No class of men can, without insulting their own nature, be content with any deprivation of their rights. We want it again, as a means for educating our race. Men are so constituted that they derive their conviction of their own possibilities largely by the estimate formed of them by others. If nothing is expected of a people, that people will find it difficult to contradict that expectation. By depriving us of suffrage, you affirm our incapacity to form an intelligent judgment respecting public men and public measures; you declare before the world that we are unfit to exercise the elective franchise, and by this means lead us to undervalue ourselves, to put a low estimate upon ourselves, and to feel that we have no possibilities like other men. Again, I want the elective franchise, for one, as a colored man, because ours is a peculiar government, based upon a peculiar idea, and that idea is universal suffrage. If I were in a monarchial government, or an autocratic or aristocratic government, where the few bore rule and the many were subject, there would be no special stigma resting upon me, because I did not exercise the elective franchise. It would do me no great violence. Mingling with the mass I should partake of the strength of the mass; I should be supported by the mass, and I should have the same incentives to endeavor with the mass of my fellow-men; it would be no particular burden, no particular deprivation; but here where universal suffrage is the rule, where that is the fundamental idea of the Government, to rule us out is to make us an exception, to brand us with the stigma of inferiority, and to invite to our heads the missiles of those about us; therefore, I want the franchise for the black man.

There are, however, other reasons, not derived from any consideration merely of our rights, but arising out of the conditions of the South, and of the country—considerations which have already been referred to by Mr. Phillips—considerations which must arrest the attention of statesmen. I believe that when the tall heads of this Rebellion shall have been swept down, as they will be swept down, when the Davises and Toombses and Stephenses, and others who are leading this Rebellion shall have been blotted out, there will be this rank undergrowth of treason, to which reference has been made, growing up there, and interfering with, and thwarting the quiet operation of the Federal Government in those states. You will see those traitors, handing down, from sire to son, the same malignant spirit which they have manifested and which they are now exhibiting, with malicious hearts, broad blades, and bloody hands in the field, against our sons and brothers. That spirit will still remain; and whoever sees the Federal Government extended over those Southern States will see that Government in a strange land, and not only in a strange land, but in an enemy's land. A postmaster of the United States in the South will find himself surrounded by a hostile spirit; a collector in a Southern port will find himself surrounded by a hostile spirit; a United States marshal or United States judge will be surrounded there by a hostile element. That enmity will not die out in a year, will not die out in an age. The Federal Government will be looked upon in those States precisely as the Governments of Austria and France are looked upon in Italy at the present moment. They will endeavor to circumvent, they will endeavor to destroy, the peaceful operation of this Government. Now, where will you find the strength to counterbalance this spirit, if you do not find it in the Negroes of the South? They are your friends, and have always been your friends. They were your friends even when the Government did not regard them as such. They comprehended the genius of this war before you did. It is a significant fact, it is a marvelous fact, it seems almost to imply a direct interposition of Providence, that this war, which began in the interest of slavery on both sides, bids fair to end in the interest of liberty on both sides. It was begun, I say, in the interest of slavery on both sides. The South was fighting to take slavery out of the Union, and the North was fighting to keep it in the Union; the South fighting to get it beyond the limits of the United States Constitution, and the North fighting to retain it within those limits; the South fighting for new guarantees, and the North fighting for the old guarantees;—both despising the Negro, both insulting the Negro. Yet, the Negro, apparently endowed with wisdom from on high, saw more clearly the end from the beginning than we did. When Seward said the status of no man in the country would be changed by the war, the Negro did not believe him. When our generals sent their underlings in shoulder-straps to hunt the flying Negro back from our lines into the jaws of slavery, from which he had escaped, the Negroes thought that a mistake had been made, and that the intentions of the Government had not been rightly understood by our officers in shoulder-straps, and they continued to come into our lines, threading their way through bogs and fens, over briers and thorns, fording streams, swimming rivers, bringing us tidings as to the safe path to march, and pointing out the dangers that threatened us. They are our only friends in the South, and we should be true to them in this, their trial hour, and see to it that they have the elective franchise.

I know that we are inferior to you in some things—virtually inferior. We walk about you like dwarfs among giants. Our heads are scarcely seen above the great sea of humanity. The Germans are superior to us; the Irish are superior to us; the Yankees are superior to us; they can do what we cannot, that is, what we have not hitherto been allowed to do. But while I make this admission, I utterly deny, that we are originally, or naturally, or practically, or in any way, or in any important sense, inferior to anybody on this globe. This charge of inferiority is an old dodge. It has been made available for oppression on many occasions. It is only about six centuries since the blue-eyed and fair-haired Anglo-Saxons were considered inferior by the haughty Normans, who once trampled upon them. If you read the history of the Norman Conquest, you will find that this proud Anglo-Saxon was once looked upon as of coarser clay than his Norman master, and might be found in the highways and byways of Old England laboring with a brass collar on his neck, and the name of his master marked upon it. You were down then! You are up now. I am glad you are up, and I want you to be glad to help us up also.

The story of our inferiority is an old dodge, as I have said; for wherever men oppress their fellows, wherever they enslave them, they will endeavor to find the needed apology for such enslavement and oppression in the character of the people oppressed and enslaved. When we wanted, a few years ago, a slice of Mexico, it was hinted that the Mexicans were an inferior race, that the old Castilian blood had become so weak that it would scarcely run down hill, and that Mexico needed the long, strong and beneficent arm of the Anglo-Saxon care extended over it. We said that it was necessary to its salvation, and a part of the "manifest destiny" of this Republic, to extend our arm over that dilapidated government. So, too, when Russia wanted to take possession of a part of the Ottoman Empire, the Turks were an "inferior race." So, too, when England wants to set the heel of her power more firmly in the quivering heart of old Ireland, the Celts are an "inferior race." So, too, the Negro, when he is to be robbed of any right which is justly his, is an "inferior man." It is said that we are ignorant; I admit it. But if we know enough to be hung, we know enough to vote. If the Negro knows enough to pay taxes to support the government, he knows enough to vote; taxation and representation should go together.

If he knows enough to shoulder a musket and fight for the flag, fight for the government, he knows enough to vote. If he knows as much when he is sober as an Irishman knows when drunk, he knows enough to vote, on good American principles.

But I was saying that you needed a counterpoise in the persons of the slaves to the enmity that would exist at the South after the Rebellion is put down. I hold that the American people are bound, not only in self-defense, to extend this right to the freedmen of the South, but they are bound by their love of country, and by all their regard for the future safety of those Southern States, to do this—to do it as a measure essential to the preservation of peace there. But I will not dwell upon this. I put it to the American sense of honor. The honor of a nation is an important thing. It is said in the Scriptures, "What doth it profit a man if he gain the whole world, and lose his own soul?" It may be said, also, What doth it profit a nation if it gain the whole world, but lose its honor? I hold that the American government has taken upon itself a solemn obligation of honor, to see that this war—let it be long or short, let it cost much or let it cost little—that this war shall not cease until every freedman at the South has the right to vote. It has bound itself to it. What have you asked the black men of the South, the black men of the whole country to do? Why, you have asked them to incur the enmity of their masters, in order to befriend you and to befriend this Government. You have asked us to call down, not only upon ourselves, but upon our children's children, the deadly hate of the entire Southern people. You have called upon us to turn our backs upon our masters, to abandon their cause and espouse yours; to turn against the South and in favor of the North; to shoot down the Confederacy and uphold the flag—the American flag. You have called upon us to expose ourselves to all the subtle machinations of their malignity for all time. And now, what do you propose to do when you come to make peace? To reward your enemies, and trample in the dust your friends? Do you intend to sacrifice the very men who have come to the rescue of your banner in the South, and incurred the lasting displeasure of their masters thereby? Do you intend to sacrifice them and reward your enemies? Do you mean to give your enemies the right to vote, and take it away from your friends? Is that wise policy? Is that honorable? Could American honor withstand such a blow? I do not believe you will do it. I think you will see to it that we have the right to vote. There is something too mean in looking upon the Negro, when you are in trouble, as a citizen, and when you are free from trouble, as an alien. When this nation was in trouble, in its early struggles, it looked upon the Negro as a citizen. In 1776 he was a citizen. At the time of the formation of the Constitution the Negro had the right to vote in eleven States out of the old thirteen. In your trouble you have made us citizens. In 1812 Gen. Jackson addressed us as citizens—"fellow-citizens." He wanted us to fight. We were citizens then! And now, when you come to frame a conscription bill, the Negro is a citizen again. He has been a citizen just three times in the history of this government, and it has always been in time of trouble. In time of trouble we are citizens. Shall we be citizens in war, and aliens in peace? Would that be just?

I ask my friends who are apologizing for not insisting upon this right, where can the black man look, in this country, for the assertion of his right, if he may not look to the Massachusetts Anti-Slavery Society? Where under the whole heavens can he look for sympathy, in asserting this right, if he may not look to this platform? Have you lifted us up to a certain height to see that we are men, and then are any disposed to leave us there, without seeing that we are put in possession of all our rights? We look naturally to this platform for the assertion of all our rights, and for this one especially. I understand the anti-slavery societies of this country to be based on two principles,—first, the freedom of the blacks of this country; and, second, the elevation of them. Let me not be misunderstood here. I am not asking for sympathy at the hands of abolitionists, sympathy at the hands of any. I think the American people are disposed often to be generous rather than just. I look over this country at the present time, and I see Educational Societies, Sanitary Commissions, Freedmen's Associations, and the like,—all very good; but in regard to the colored people there is always more that is benevolent, I perceive, than just, manifested towards us. What I ask for the Negro is not benevolence, not pity, not sympathy, but simply justice. The American people have always been anxious to know what they shall do with us. Gen. Banks was distressed with solicitude as to what he should do with the Negro. Everybody has asked the question, and they learned to ask it early of the abolitionists, "What shall we do with the Negro?" I have had but one answer from the beginning. Do nothing with us! Your doing with us has already played the mischief with us. Do nothing with us! If the apples will not remain on the tree of their own strength, if they are worm-eaten at the core, if they are early ripe and disposed to fall, let them fall! I am not for tying or fastening them on the tree in any way, except by nature's plan, and if they will not stay there, let them fall. And if the Negro cannot stand on his own legs, let him fall also. All I ask is, give him a chance to stand on his own legs! Let him alone! If you see him on his way to school, let him alone, don't disturb him! If you see him going to the dinner table at a hotel, let him go! If you see him going to the ballot-box, let him alone, don't disturb him! If you see him going into a work-shop, just let him alone,—your interference is doing him a positive injury. Gen. Banks' "preparation" is of a piece with this attempt to prop up the Negro. Let him fall if he cannot stand alone! If the Negro cannot live by the line of eternal justice, so beautifully pictured to you in the illustration used by Mr. Phillips, the fault will not be yours, it will be his who made the Negro, and established that line for his government. [Applause.] Let him live or die by that. If you will only untie his hands, and give him a chance, I think he will live. He will work as readily for himself as the white man. A great many delusions have been swept away by this war. One was, that the Negro would not work; he has proved his ability to work. Another was, that the Negro would not fight; that he possessed only the most sheepish attributes of humanity; was a perfect lamb, or an "Uncle Tom;" disposed to take off his coat whenever required, fold his hands, and be whipped by anybody who wanted to whip him. But the war has proved that there is a great deal of human nature in the Negro, and that "he will fight," as Mr. Quincy, our President, said, in earlier days than these, "when there is reasonable probability of his whipping anybody."

Oration in Memory of Abraham Lincoln
(1876)

Frederick Douglass had gotten to know Abraham Lincoln over the course of the civil war, first by helping the President to recruit African American troops for the Union Army, and eventually, after meeting on several occasions, being invited as the only non-white guest to Lincoln's second inauguration. The following speech was delivered at the unveiling of the Lincoln Memorial statue on April 14, 1876.

Friends and Fellow-Citizens.

I warmly congratulate you upon the highly interesting object which has caused you to assemble in such numbers and spirit as you have today. This occasion is in some respects remarkable. Wise and thoughtful men of our race, who shall come after us, and study the lesson of our history in the United States; who shall survey the long and dreary spaces over which we have traveled; who shall count the links in the great chain of events by which we have reached our present position, will make a note of this occasion; they will think of it and speak of it with a sense of manly pride and complacency.

I congratulate you, also, upon the very favorable circumstances in which we meet today. They are high, inspiring, and uncommon. They lend grace, glory, and significance to the object for which we have met. Nowhere else in this great country, with its uncounted towns and cities, unlimited wealth, and immeasurable territory extending from sea to sea, could conditions be found more favorable to the success of this occasion than here.

We stand today at the national center to perform something like a national act—an act which is to go into history; and we are here where every pulsation of the national heart can be heard, felt, and reciprocated. A thousand wires, fed with thought and winged with lightning, put us in instantaneous communication with the loyal and true men all over the country.

Few facts could better illustrate the vast and wonderful change which has taken place in our condition as a people than the fact of our assembling here for the purpose we have today. Harmless, beautiful, proper, and praiseworthy as this demonstration is, I cannot forget that no such demonstration would have been tolerated here twenty years ago. The spirit of slavery and barbarism, which still lingers to blight and destroy in some dark and distant parts of our country, would have made our assembling here the signal and excuse for opening upon us all the flood-gates of wrath and violence. That we are here in peace today is a compliment and a credit to American civilization, and a prophecy of still greater national enlightenment and progress in the future. I refer to the past not in malice, for this is no day for malice; but simply to place more distinctly in front the gratifying and glorious change which has come both to our white fellow-citizens and ourselves, and to congratulate all upon the contrast between now and then; the new dispensation of freedom with its thousand blessings to both races, and the old dispensation of slavery with its ten thousand evils to both races—white and black. In view, then, of the past, the present, and the future, with the long and dark history of our bondage behind us, and with liberty, progress, and enlightenment before us, I again congratulate you upon this auspicious day and hour.

Friends and fellow-citizens, the story of our presence here is soon and easily told. We are here in the District of Columbia, here in the city of Washington, the most luminous point of American territory; a city recently transformed and made beautiful in its body and in its spirit; we are here in the place where the ablest and best men of the country are sent to devise the policy, enact the laws, and shape the destiny of the Republic; we are here, with the stately pillars and majestic dome of the Capitol of the nation looking down upon us; we are here, with the broad earth freshly adorned with the foliage and flowers of spring for our church, and all races, colors, and conditions of men for our congregation—in a word, we are here to express, as best we may, by appropriate forms and ceremonies, our grateful sense of the vast, high, and preeminent services rendered to ourselves, to our race, to our country, and to the whole world by Abraham Lincoln.

The sentiment that brings us here today is one of the noblest that can stir and thrill the human heart. It has crowned and made glorious the high places of all civilized nations with the grandest and most enduring works of art, designed to illustrate the characters and perpetuate the memories of great public men. It is the sentiment which from year to year adorns with fragrant and beautiful flowers the graves of our loyal, brave, and patriotic soldiers who fell in defense of the Union and liberty. It is the sentiment of gratitude and appreciation, which often, in the presence of many who hear me, has filled yonder heights of Arlington with the eloquence of eulogy and the sublime enthusiasm of poetry and song; a sentiment which can never die while the Republic lives.

For the first time in the history of our people, and in the history of the whole American people, we join in this high worship, and march conspicuously in the line of this time-honored custom. First things are always interesting, and this is one of our first things. It is the first time that, in this form and manner, we have sought to do honor to an American great man, however deserving and illustrious. I commend the fact to notice; let it be told in every part of the Republic; let men of all parties and opinions hear it; let those who despise us, not less than those who respect us, know that now and here, in the spirit of liberty, loyalty, and gratitude, let it be known everywhere, and by everybody who takes an interest in human progress and in the amelioration of the condition of mankind, that, in the presence and with the approval of the members of the American House of Representatives, reflecting the general sentiment of the country; that in the presence of that august body, the American Senate, representing the highest intelligence and the calmest judgment of the country; in the presence of the Supreme Court and Chief-Justice of the United States, to whose decisions we all patriotically bow; in the presence and under the steady eye of the honored and trusted Cabinet, we, the colored people, newly emancipated and rejoicing in our blood-bought freedom, near the close of the first century in the life of this Republic, have now and here unveiled, set apart, and dedicated a figure of which the men of this generation may read, and those of after-coming generations may read, something of the exalted character and great works of Abraham Lincoln, the first martyr President of the United States.

Fellow-citizens, in what we have said and done today, and in what we may say and do hereafter, we disclaim everything like arrogance and assumption. We claim for ourselves no superior devotion to the character, history, and memory of the illustrious name whose monument we have here dedicated today. We fully comprehend the relation of Abraham Lincoln both to ourselves and to the white people of the United States. Truth is proper and beautiful at all times and in all places, and it is never more proper and beautiful in any case than when speaking of a great public man whose example is likely to be commended for honor and imitation long after his departure to the solemn shades, the silent continents of eternity. It must be admitted, truth compels me to admit, even here in the presence of the monument we have erected to his memory, Abraham Lincoln was not, in the fullest sense of the word, either our man or our model. In his interests, in his associations, in his habits of thought, and in his prejudices, he was a white man.

He was preeminently the white man's President, entirely devoted to the welfare of white men. He was ready and willing at any time during the first years of his administration to deny, postpone, and sacrifice the rights of humanity in the colored people to promote the welfare of the white people of this country. In all his education and feeling he was an American of the Americans. He came into the Presidential chair upon one principle alone, namely, opposition to the extension of slavery. His arguments in furtherance of this policy had their motive and mainspring in his patriotic devotion to the interests of his own race. To protect, defend, and perpetuate slavery in the states where it existed Abraham Lincoln was not less ready than any other President to draw the sword of the nation. He was ready to execute all the supposed guarantees of the United States Constitution in favor of the slave system anywhere inside the slave states. He was willing to pursue, recapture, and send back the fugitive slave to his master, and to suppress a slave rising for liberty, though his guilty master were already in arms against the Government. The race to which we belong were not the special objects of his consideration. Knowing this, I concede to you, my white fellow-citizens, a pre-eminence in this worship at once full and supreme. First, midst, and last, you and yours were the objects of his deepest affection and his most earnest solicitude. You are the children of Abraham Lincoln. We are at best only his step-children; children by adoption, children by forces of circumstances and necessity. To you it especially belongs to sound his praises, to preserve and perpetuate his memory, to multiply his statues, to hang his pictures high upon your walls, and commend his example, for to you he was a great and glorious friend and benefactor. Instead of supplanting you at his altar, we would exhort you to build high his monuments; let them be of the most costly material, of the most cunning workmanship; let their forms be symmetrical, beautiful, and perfect, let their bases be upon solid rocks, and their summits lean against the unchanging blue, overhanging sky, and let them endure forever! But while in the abundance of your wealth, and in the fullness of your just and patriotic devotion, you do all this, we entreat you to despise not the humble offering we this day unveil to view; for while Abraham Lincoln saved for you a country, he delivered us from a bondage, according to Jefferson, one hour of which was worse than ages of the oppression your fathers rose in rebellion to oppose.

Fellow-citizens, ours is no new-born zeal and devotion—merely a thing of this moment. The name of Abraham Lincoln was near and dear to our hearts in the darkest and most perilous hours of the Republic. We were no more ashamed of him when shrouded in clouds of darkness, of doubt, and defeat than when we saw him crowned with victory, honor, and glory. Our faith in him was often taxed and strained to the uttermost, but it never failed. When he tarried long in the mountain; when he strangely told us that we were the cause of the war; when he still more strangely told us that we were to leave the land in which we were born; when he refused to employ our arms in defense of the Union; when, after accepting our services as colored soldiers, he refused to retaliate our murder and torture as colored prisoners; when he told us he would save the Union if he could with slavery; when he revoked the Proclamation of Emancipation of General Fremont; when he refused to remove the popular commander of the Army of the Potomac, in the days of its inaction and defeat, who was more zealous in his efforts to protect slavery than to suppress rebellion; when we saw all this, and more, we were at times grieved, stunned, and greatly bewildered; but our hearts believed while they ached and bled. Nor was this, even at that time, a blind and unreasoning superstition. Despite the mist and haze that surrounded him; despite the tumult, the hurry, and confusion of the hour, we were able to take a comprehensive view of Abraham Lincoln, and to make reasonable allowance for the circumstances of his position. We saw him, measured him, and estimated him; not by stray utterances to injudicious and tedious delegations, who often tried his patience; not by isolated facts torn from their connection; not by any partial and imperfect glimpses, caught at inopportune moments; but by a broad survey, in the light of the stern logic of great events, and in view of that divinity which shapes our ends, rough hew them how we will, we came to the conclusion that the hour and the man of our redemption had somehow met in the person of Abraham Lincoln. It mattered little to us what language he might employ on special occasions; it mattered little to us, when we fully knew him, whether he was swift or slow in his movements; it was enough for us that Abraham Lincoln was at the head of a great movement, and was in living and earnest sympathy with that movement, which, in the nature of things, must go on until slavery should be utterly and forever abolished in the United States.

When, therefore, it shall be asked what we have to do with the memory of Abraham Lincoln, or what Abraham Lincoln had to do with us, the answer is ready, full, and complete. Though he loved Caesar less than Rome, though the Union was more to him than our freedom or our future, under his wise and beneficent rule we saw ourselves gradually lifted from the depths of slavery to the heights of liberty and manhood; under his wise and beneficent rule, and by measures approved and vigorously pressed by him, we saw that the handwriting of ages, in the form of prejudice and proscription, was rapidly fading away from the face of our whole country; under his rule, and in due time, about as soon after all as the country could tolerate the strange spectacle, we saw our brave sons and brothers laying off the rags of bondage, and being clothed all over in the blue uniforms of the soldiers of the United States; under his rule we saw two hundred thousand of our dark and dusky people responding to the call of Abraham Lincoln, and with muskets on their shoulders, and eagles on their buttons, timing their high footsteps to liberty and union under the national flag; under his rule we saw the independence of the black republic of Haiti, the special object of slaveholding aversion and horror, fully recognized, and her minister, a colored gentleman, duly received here in the city of Washington; under his rule we saw the internal slave-trade, which so long disgraced the nation, abolished, and slavery abolished in the District of Columbia; under his rule we saw for the first time the law enforced against the foreign slave-trade, and the first slave-trader hanged like any other pirate or murderer; under his rule, assisted by the greatest captain of our age, and his inspiration, we saw the Confederate States, based upon the idea that our race must be slaves, and slaves forever, battered to pieces and scattered to the four winds; under his rule, and in the fullness of time, we saw Abraham Lincoln, after giving the slaveholders three months' grace in which to save their hateful slave system, penning the immortal paper, which, though special in its language, was general in its principles and effect, making slavery forever impossible in the United States. Though we waited long, we saw all this and more.

Can any colored man, or any white man friendly to the freedom of all men, ever forget the night which followed the first day of January, 1863, when the world was to see if Abraham Lincoln would prove to be as good as his word? I shall never forget that memorable night, when in a distant city I waited and watched at a public meeting, with three thousand others not less anxious than myself, for the word of deliverance which we have heard read today. Nor shall I ever forget the outburst of joy and thanksgiving that rent the air when the lightning brought to us the emancipation proclamation. In that happy hour we forgot all delay, and forgot all tardiness, forgot that the President had bribed the rebels to lay down their arms by a promise to withhold the bolt which would smite the slave-system with destruction; and we were thenceforward willing to allow the President all the latitude of time, phraseology, and every honorable device that statesmanship might require for the achievement of a great and beneficent measure of liberty and progress.

Fellow-citizens, there is little necessity on this occasion to speak at length and critically of this great and good man, and of his high mission in the world. That ground has been fully occupied and completely covered both here and elsewhere. The whole field of fact and fancy has been gleaned and garnered. Any man can say things that are true of Abraham Lincoln, but no man can say anything that is new of Abraham Lincoln. His personal traits and public acts are better known to the American people than are those of any other man of his age. He was a mystery to no man who saw him and heard him. Though high in position, the humblest could approach him and feel at home in his presence. Though deep, he was transparent; though strong, he was gentle; though decided and pronounced in his convictions, he was tolerant towards those who differed from him, and patient under reproaches. Even those who only knew him through his public utterance obtained a tolerably clear idea of his character and personality. The image of the man went out with his words, and those who read them knew him.

I have said that President Lincoln was a white man, and shared the prejudices common to his countrymen towards the colored race. Looking back to his times and to the condition of his country, we are compelled to admit that this unfriendly feeling on his part may be safely set down as one element of his wonderful success in organizing the loyal American people for the tremendous conflict before them, and bringing them safely through that conflict. His great mission was to accomplish two things: first, to save his country from dismemberment and ruin; and, second, to free his country from the great crime of slavery. To do one or the other, or both, he must have the earnest sympathy and the powerful cooperation of his loyal fellow-countrymen. Without this primary and essential condition to success his efforts must have been vain and utterly fruitless. Had he put the abolition of slavery before the salvation of the Union, he would have inevitably driven from him a powerful class of the American people and rendered resistance to rebellion impossible. Viewed from the genuine abolition ground, Mr. Lincoln seemed tardy, cold, dull, and indifferent; but measuring him by the sentiment of his country, a sentiment he was bound as a statesman to consult, he was swift, zealous, radical, and determined.

Though Mr. Lincoln shared the prejudices of his white fellow-countrymen against the Negro, it is hardly necessary to say that in his heart of hearts he loathed and hated slavery. The man who could say, "Fondly do we hope, fervently do we pray, that this mighty scourge of war shall soon pass away, yet if God wills it continue till all the wealth piled by two hundred years of bondage shall have been wasted, and each drop of blood drawn by the lash shall have been paid for by one drawn by the sword, the judgments of the Lord are true and righteous altogether," gives all needed proof of his feeling on the subject of slavery. He was willing, while the South was loyal, that it should have its pound of flesh, because he thought that it was so nominated in the bond; but farther than this no earthly power could make him go.

Fellow-citizens, whatever else in this world may be partial, unjust, and uncertain, time, time! is impartial, just, and certain in its action. In the realm of mind, as well as in the realm of matter, it is a great worker, and often works wonders. The honest and comprehensive statesman, clearly discerning the needs of his country, and earnestly endeavoring to do his whole duty, though covered and blistered with reproaches, may safely leave his course to the silent judgment of time. Few great public men have ever been the victims of fiercer denunciation than Abraham Lincoln was during his administration. He was often wounded in the house of his friends. Reproaches came thick and fast upon him from within and from without, and from opposite quarters. He was assailed by Abolitionists; he was assailed by slaveholders; he was assailed by the men who were for peace at any price; he was assailed by those who were for a more vigorous prosecution of the war; he was assailed for not making the war an abolition war; and he was bitterly assailed for making the war an abolition war.

But now behold the change: the judgment of the present hour is, that taking him for all in all, measuring the tremendous magnitude of the work before him, considering the necessary means to ends, and surveying the end from the beginning, infinite wisdom has seldom sent any man into the world better fitted for his mission than Abraham Lincoln. His birth, his training, and his natural endowments, both mental and physical, were strongly in his favor. Born and reared among the lowly, a stranger to wealth and luxury, compelled to grapple single-handed with the flintiest hardships of life, from tender youth to sturdy manhood, he grew strong in the manly and heroic qualities demanded by the great mission to which he was called by the votes of his countrymen. The hard condition of his early life, which would have depressed and broken down weaker men, only gave greater life, vigor, and buoyancy to the heroic spirit of Abraham Lincoln. He was ready for any kind and any quality of work. What other young men dreaded in the shape of toil, he took hold of with the utmost cheerfulness.

"A spade, a rake, a hoe,
A pick-axe, or a bill;
A hook to reap, a scythe to mow,
A flail, or what you will."

All day long he could split heavy rails in the woods, and half the night long he could study his English Grammar by the uncertain flare and glare of the light made by a pine-knot. He was at home in the land with his axe, with his maul, with gluts, and his wedges; and he was equally at home on water, with his oars, with his poles, with his planks, and with his boat-hooks. And whether in his flat-boat on the Mississippi River, or at the fireside of his frontier cabin, he was a man of work. A son of toil himself, he was linked in brotherly sympathy with the sons of toil in every loyal part of the Republic. This very fact gave him tremendous power with the American people, and materially contributed not only to selecting him to the Presidency, but in sustaining his administration of the Government.

Upon his inauguration as President of the United States, an office, even when assumed under the most favorable condition, fitted to tax and strain the largest abilities, Abraham Lincoln was met by a tremendous crisis. He was called upon not merely to administer the Government, but to decide, in the face of terrible odds, the fate of the Republic.

A formidable rebellion rose in his path before him; the Union was already practically dissolved; his country was torn and rent asunder at the center. Hostile armies were already organized against the Republic, armed with the munitions of war which the Republic had provided for its own defense. The tremendous question for him to decide was whether his country should survive the crisis and flourish, or be dismembered and perish. His predecessor in office had already decided the question in favor of national dismemberment, by denying to it the right of self-defense and self-preservation—a right which belongs to the meanest insect.

Happily for the country, happily for you and for me, the judgment of James Buchanan, the patrician, was not the judgment of Abraham Lincoln, the plebeian. He brought his strong common sense, sharpened in the school of adversity, to bear upon the question. He did not hesitate, he did not doubt, he did not falter; but at once resolved that at whatever peril, at whatever cost, the union of the States should be preserved. A patriot himself, his faith was strong and unwavering in the patriotism of his countrymen. Timid men said before Mr. Lincoln's inauguration, that we have seen the last President of the United States. A voice in influential quarters said, "Let the Union slide." Some said that a Union maintained by the sword was worthless. Others said a rebellion of 8,000,000 cannot be suppressed; but in the midst of all this tumult and timidity, and against all this, Abraham Lincoln was clear in his duty, and had an oath in heaven. He calmly and bravely heard the voice of doubt and fear all around him; but he had an oath in heaven, and there was not power enough on earth to make this honest boatman, backwoodsman, and broad-handed splitter of rails evade or violate that sacred oath. He had not been schooled in the ethics of slavery; his plain life had favored his love of truth. He had not been taught that treason and perjury were the proof of honor and honesty. His moral training was against his saying one thing when he meant another. The trust that Abraham Lincoln had in himself and in the people was surprising and grand, but it was also enlightened and well founded. He knew the American people better than they knew themselves, and his truth was based upon this knowledge.

Fellow-citizens, the fourteenth day of April, 1865, of which this is the eleventh anniversary, is now and will ever remain a memorable day in the annals of this Republic. It was on the evening of this day, while a fierce and sanguinary rebellion was in the last stages of its desolating power; while its armies were broken and scattered before the invincible armies of Grant and Sherman; while a great nation, torn and rent by war, was already beginning to raise to the skies loud anthems of joy at the dawn of peace, it was startled, amazed, and overwhelmed by the crowning crime of slavery—the assassination of Abraham Lincoln. It was a new crime, a pure act of malice. No purpose of the rebellion was to be served by it. It was the simple gratification of a hell-black spirit of revenge. But it has done good after all. It has filled the country with a deeper abhorrence of slavery and a deeper love for the great liberator.

Had Abraham Lincoln died from any of the numerous ills to which flesh is heir; had he reached that good old age of which his vigorous constitution and his temperate habits gave promise; had he been permitted to see the end of his great work; had the solemn curtain of death come down but gradually—we should still have been smitten with a heavy grief, and treasured his name lovingly. But dying as he did die, by the red hand of violence, killed, assassinated, taken off without warning, not because of personal hate—for no man who knew Abraham Lincoln could hate him—but because of his fidelity to union and liberty, he is doubly dear to us, and his memory will be precious forever.

Fellow-citizens, I end, as I began, with congratulations. We have done a good work for our race today. In doing honor to the memory of our friend and liberator, we have been doing highest honors to ourselves and those who come after us; we have been fastening ourselves to a name and fame imperishable and immortal; we have also been defending ourselves from a blighting scandal. When now it shall be said that the colored man is soulless, that he has no appreciation of benefits or benefactors; when the foul reproach of ingratitude is hurled at us, and it is attempted to scourge us beyond the range of human brotherhood, we may calmly point to the monument we have this day erected to the memory of Abraham Lincoln.

John Brown
(1881)

John Brown gained notoriety throughout the 1850s as a revolutionary abolition-
ist who advocated armed rebellion as a means for ending the practice of slavery
in the United States. He was executed shortly after leading 18 men on a raid of
the Harpers Ferry Armory in 1859. In the following speech, delivered on May
30, 1881 at the Fourteenth Anniversary of Storer College, Douglass discusses
the lasting impact of John Brown's life on the history of Slavery in America.

Not to fan the flame of sectional animosity now happily in the process
of rapid and I hope permanent extinction, not to revive and keep alive
a sense of shame and remorse for a great national crime, which has
brought its own punishment, in loss of treasure, tears and blood, not
to recount the long list of wrongs, inflicted on my race during more
than two hundred years of merciless bondage; nor yet to draw, from the
labyrinths of far-off centuries, incidents and achievements wherewith
to rouse your passions, and enkindle your enthusiasm, but to pay a just
debt long due, to vindicate in some degree a great historical character,
of our own time and country, one with whom I was myself well acquainted, and whose friendship and confidence it was my good fortune
to share, and to give you such recollections, impressions and facts, as I
can, of a grand, brave and good old man, and especially to promote a
better understanding of the raid upon Harper's Ferry of which he was
the chief, is the object of this address.

In all the thirty years' conflict with slavery, if we except the late tremendous war, there is no subject which in its interest and importance
will be remembered longer, or will form a more thrilling chapter in
American history than this strange, wild, bloody and mournful drama.
The story of it is still fresh in the minds of many who now hear me, but
for the sake of those who may have forgotten its details, and in order to
have our subject in its entire range more fully and clearly before us at
the outset, I will briefly state the facts in that extraordinary transaction.

On the night of the 16th of October, 1859, there appeared near the confluence of the Potomac and Shenandoah rivers, a party of nineteen men—fourteen white and five colored. They were not only armed themselves, but had brought with them a large supply of arms for such persons as might join them. These men invaded Harper's Ferry, disarmed the watchman, took possession of the arsenal, rifle-factory, armory and other government property at that place, arrested and made prisoners nearly all the prominent citizens of the neighborhood, collected about fifty slaves, put bayonets into the hands of such as were able and willing to fight for their liberty, killed three men, proclaimed general emancipation, held the ground more than thirty hours, were subsequently overpowered and nearly all killed, wounded or captured, by a body of United States troops, under command of Colonel Robert E. Lee, since famous as the rebel Gen. Lee. Three out of the nineteen invaders were captured whilst fighting, and one of these was Captain John Brown, the man who originated, planned and commanded the expedition. At the time of his capture Capt. Brown was supposed to be mortally wounded, as he had several ugly gashes and bayonet wounds on his head and body; and apprehending that he might speedily die, or that he might be rescued by his friends, and thus the opportunity of making him a signal example of slaveholding vengeance would be lost, his captors hurried him to Charlestown two miles further within the border of Virginia, placed him in prison strongly guarded by troops, and before his wounds were healed he was brought into court, subjected to a nominal trial, convicted of high treason and inciting slaves to insurrection, and was executed. His corpse was given to his woe-stricken widow, and she, assisted by Antislavery friends, caused it to be borne to North Elba, Essex County, NY, and there his dust now reposes, amid the silent, solemn and snowy grandeur of the Adirondacks.

Such is the story; with no line softened or hardened to my inclining. It certainly is not a story to please, but to pain. It is not a story to increase our sense of social safety and security, but to fill the imagination with wild and troubled fancies of doubt and danger. It was a sudden and startling surprise to the people of Harper's Ferry, and it is not easy to conceive of a situation more abundant in all the elements of horror and consternation. They had retired as usual to rest, with no suspicion that an enemy lurked in the surrounding darkness. They had quietly and trustingly given themselves up to "tired Nature's sweet restorer, balmy sleep," and while thus all unconscious of danger, they were roused from their peaceful slumbers by the sharp crack of the invader's rifle, and felt the keen-edged sword of war at their throats, three of their number being already slain.

Every feeling of the human heart was naturally outraged at this occurrence, and hence at the moment the air was full of denunciation and
execration. So intense was this feeling, that few ventured to whisper a
word of apology. But happily reason has her voice as well as feeling, and
though slower in deciding, her judgments are broader, deeper, clearer
and more enduring. It is not easy to reconcile human feeling to the
shedding of blood for any purpose, unless indeed in the excitement
which the shedding of blood itself occasions. The knife is to feeling
always an offence. Even when in the hands of a skillful surgeon, it refuses consent to the operation long after reason has demonstrated its
necessity. It even pleads the cause of the known murderer on the day
of his execution, and calls society half criminal when, in cold blood, it
takes life as a protection of itself from crime. Let no word be said against
this holy feeling; more than to law and government are we indebted
to this tender sentiment of regard for human life for the safety with
which we walk the streets by day and sleep secure in our beds at night.
It is nature's grand police, vigilant and faithful, sentineled in the soul,
guarding against violence to peace and life. But whilst so much is freely
accorded to feeling in the economy of human welfare, something more
than feeling is necessary to grapple with a fact so grim and significant
as was this raid. Viewed apart and alone, as a transaction separate and
distinct from its antecedents and bearings, it takes rank with the most
cold-blooded and atrocious wrongs ever perpetrated; but just here is
the trouble—this raid on Harper's Ferry, no more than Sherman's
march to the sea can consent to be thus viewed alone.

There is, in the world's government, a force which has in all ages
been recognized, sometimes as Nemesis, sometimes as the judgment
of God and sometimes as retributive justice; but under whatever name,
all history attests the wisdom and beneficence of its chastisements, and
men become reconciled to the agents through whom it operates, and
have extolled them as heroes, benefactors and demigods.

To the broad vision of a true philosophy, nothing in this world stands
alone. Everything is a necessary part of everything else. The margin of
chance is narrowed by every extension of reason and knowledge, and
nothing comes unbidden to the feast of human experience. The universe, of which we are a part, is continually proving itself a stupendous
whole, a system of law and order, eternal and perfect. Every seed bears
fruit after its kind, and nothing is reaped which was not sowed. The
distance between seed time and harvest, in the moral world, may not
be quite so well defined or as clearly intelligible as in the physical, but
there is a seed time, and there is a harvest time, and though ages may
intervene, and neither he who ploughed nor he who sowed may reap

in person, yet the harvest nevertheless will surely come, and as in the physical world there are century plants, so it may be in the moral world, and their fruitage is as certain in the one as in the other. The bloody harvest of Harper's Ferry was ripened by the heat and moisture of merciless bondage of more than two hundred years. That startling cry of alarm on the banks of the Potomac was but the answering back of the avenging angel to the midnight invasions of Christian slave-traders on the sleeping hamlets of Africa. The history of the African slave-trade furnishes many illustrations far more cruel and bloody.

Viewed thus broadly our subject is worthy of thoughtful and dispassionate consideration. It invites the study of the poet, scholar, philosopher and statesman. What the masters in natural science have done for man in the physical world, the masters of social science may yet do for him in the moral world. Science now tells us when storms are in the sky, and when and where their violence will be most felt. Why may we not yet know with equal certainty when storms are in the moral sky, and how to avoid their desolating force? But I can invite you to no such profound discussions. I am not the man, nor is this the occasion for such philosophical enquiry. Mine is the word of grateful memory to an old friend; to tell you what I knew of him—what I knew of his inner life—of what he did and what he attempted, and thus if possible to make the mainspring of his actions manifest and thereby give you a clearer view of his character and services.

It is said that next in value to the performance of great deeds ourselves, is the capacity to appreciate such when performed by others; to more than this I do not presume. Allow me one other personal word before I proceed. In the minds of some of the American people I was myself credited with an important agency in the John Brown raid. Governor Henry A. Wise was manifestly of that opinion. He was at the pains of having Mr. Buchanan send his Marshals to Rochester to invite me to accompany them to Virginia. Fortunately I left town several hours previous to their arrival.

What ground there was for this distinguished consideration shall duly appear in the natural course of this lecture. I wish however to say just here that there was no foundation whatever for the charge that I in any wise urged or instigated John Brown to his dangerous work. I rejoice that it is my good fortune to have seen, not only the end of slavery, but to see the day when the whole truth can be told about this matter without prejudice to either the living or the dead. I shall however allow myself little prominence in these disclosures. Your interests, like mine, are in the all-commanding figure of the story, and to him I consecrate the hour. His zeal in the cause of my race was far greater than mine—it was as the burning sun to my taper light—mine was bounded by time, his stretched away to the boundless shores of eternity. I could live for the slave, but he could die for him. The crown of martyrdom is high, far beyond the reach of ordinary mortals, and yet happily no special greatness or superior moral excellence is necessary to discern and in some measure appreciate a truly great soul. Cold, calculating and unspiritual as most of us are, we are not wholly insensible to real greatness; and when we are brought in contact with a man of commanding mold, towering high and alone above the millions, free from all conventional fetters, true to his own moral convictions, a "law unto himself," ready to suffer misconstruction, ignoring torture and death for what he believes to be right, we are compelled to do him homage.

In the stately shadow, in the sublime presence of such a soul I find myself standing to-night; and how to do it reverence, how to do it justice, how to honor the dead with due regard to the living, has been a matter of most anxious solicitude.

Much has been said of John Brown, much that is wise and beautiful, but in looking over what may be called the John Brown literature, I have been little assisted with material, and even less encouraged with any hope of success in treating the subject. Scholarship, genius and devotion have hastened with poetry and eloquence, story and song to this simple altar of human virtue, and have retired dissatisfied and distressed with the thinness and poverty of their offerings, as I shall with mine.

The difficulty in doing justice to the life and character of such a man is not altogether due to the quality of the zeal, or of the ability brought to the work, nor yet to any imperfections in the qualities of the man himself; the state of the moral atmosphere about us has much to do with it. The fault is not in our eyes, nor yet in the object, if under a murky sky we fail to discover the object. Wonderfully tenacious is the taint of a great wrong. The evil, as well as "the good that men do, lives after them." Slavery is indeed gone; but its long, black shadow yet falls broad and large over the face of the whole country. It is the old truth oft repeated, and never more fitly than now, "a prophet is without honor in his own country and among his own people." Though more than twenty years have rolled between us and the Harper's Ferry raid, though since then the armies of the nation have found it necessary to do on a large scale what John Brown attempted to do on a small one, and the great captain who fought his way through slavery has filled with honor the Presidential chair, we yet stand too near the days of slavery, and the life and times of John Brown, to see clearly the true martyr and hero that he was and rightly to estimate the value of the man and his works. Like the great and good of all ages—the men born in advance of their times, the men whose bleeding footprints attest the immense cost of reform, and show us the long and dreary spaces, between the luminous points in the progress of mankind,—this our noblest American hero must wait the polishing wheels of after-coming centuries to make his glory more manifest, and his worth more generally acknowledged. Such instances are abundant and familiar. If we go back four and twenty centuries, to the stately city of Athens, and search among her architectural splendor and her miracles of art for the Socrates of today, and as he stands in history, we shall find ourselves perplexed and disappointed. In Jerusalem Jesus himself was only the "carpenter's son"—a young man wonderfully destitute of worldly prudence—a pestilent fellow, "inexcusably and perpetually interfering in the world's business,"—"upsetting the tables of the money-changers"—preaching sedition, opposing the good old religion—"making himself greater than Abraham," and at the same time "keeping company" with very low people; but behold the change! He was a great miracle-worker, in his day, but time has worked for him a greater miracle than all his miracles, for now his name stands for all that is desirable in government, noble in life, orderly and beautiful in society. That which time has done for other great men of his class, that will time certainly do for John Brown. The brightest gems shine at first with subdued light, and the strongest characters are subject to the same limitations. Under the influence of adverse education and hereditary bias, few things are more difficult than to render impartial justice. Men hold up their hands to Heaven, and swear they will do justice, but what are oaths against prejudice and against inclination! In the face of high-sounding professions and affirmations we know well how hard it is for a Turk to do justice to a Christian, or for a Christian to do justice to a Jew. How hard for an Englishman to do justice to an Irishman, for an Irishman to do justice to an Englishman, harder still for an American tainted by slavery to do justice to the Negro or the Negro's friends. "John Brown," said the late Wm. H. Seward, "was justly hanged." "John Brown," said the late John A. Andrew, "was right." It is easy to perceive the sources of these two opposite judgments: the one was the verdict of slaveholding and panic-stricken Virginia, the other was the verdict of the best heart and brain of free old Massachusetts. One was the heated judgment of the passing and passionate hour, and the other was the calm, clear, unimpeachable judgment of the broad, illimitable future.

There is, however, one aspect of the present subject quite worthy of notice, for it makes the hero of Harper's Ferry in some degree an exception to the general rules to which I have just now adverted. Despite the hold which slavery had at that time on the country, despite the popular prejudice against the Negro, despite the shock which the first alarm occasioned, almost from the first John Brown received a large measure of sympathy and appreciation. New England recognized in him the spirit which brought the pilgrims to Plymouth rock and hailed him as a martyr and saint. True he had broken the law, true he had struck for a despised people, true he had crept upon his foe stealthily, like a wolf upon the fold, and had dealt his blow in the dark whilst his enemy slept, but with all this and more to disturb the moral sense, men discerned in him the greatest and best qualities known to human nature, and pronounced him "good." Many consented to his death, and then went home and taught their children to sing his praise as one whose "soul is marching on" through the realms of endless bliss. One element in explanation of this somewhat anomalous circumstance will probably be found in the troubled times which immediately succeeded, for "when judgments are abroad in the world, men learn righteousness."

The country had before this learned the value of Brown's heroic character. He had shown boundless courage and skill in dealing with the enemies of liberty in Kansas. With men so few, and means so small, and odds against him so great, no captain ever surpassed him in achievements, some of which seem almost beyond belief. With only eight men in that bitter war, he met, fought and captured Henry Clay Pate, with twenty-five well armed and mounted men. In this memorable encounter, he selected his ground so wisely, handled his men so skillfully, and attacked the enemy so vigorously, that they could neither run nor fight, and were therefore compelled to surrender to a force less than one-third their own. With just thirty men on another important occasion during the same border war, he met and vanquished four hundred Missourians under the command of Gen. Read. These men had come into the territory under an oath never to return to their homes till they had stamped out the last vestige of free State spirit in Kansas; but a brush with old Brown took this high conceit out of them, and they were glad to get off upon any terms, without stopping to stipulate. With less than one hundred men to defend the town of Lawrence, he offered to lead them and give battle to fourteen hundred men on the banks of the Waukerusia [sic] river, and was much vexed when his offer was refused by Gen. Jim Lane and others to whom the defense of the town was confided. Before leaving Kansas, he went into the border of Missouri, and liberated a dozen slaves in a single night, and, in spite of slave laws and marshals, he brought these people through a half dozen States, and landed them safely in Canada. With eighteen men this man shook the whole social fabric of Virginia. With eighteen men he overpowered a town of nearly three thousand souls. With these eighteen men he held that large community firmly in his grasp for thirty long hours. With these eighteen men he rallied in a single night fifty slaves to his standard, and made prisoners of an equal number of the slaveholding class. With these eighteen men he defied the power and bravery of a dozen of the best militia companies that Virginia could send against him. Now, when slavery struck, as it certainly did strike, at the life of the country, it was not the fault of John Brown that our rulers did not at first know how to deal with it. He had already shown us the weak side of the rebellion, had shown us where to strike and how. It was not from lack of native courage that Virginia submitted for thirty long hours and at last was relieved only by Federal troops, but because the attack was made on the side of her conscience and thus armed her against herself. She beheld at her side the sullen brow of a black Ireland. When John Brown proclaimed emancipation to the slaves of Maryland and Virginia he added to his war power the force of a moral earthquake. Virginia felt all her strong-ribbed mountains to shake under the heavy tread of armed insurgents. Of his army of nineteen her conscience made an army of nineteen hundred.

Another feature of the times, worthy of notice, was the effect of this blow upon the country at large. At the first moment we were stunned and bewildered. Slavery had so benumbed the moral sense of the nation, that it never suspected the possibility of an explosion like this, and it was difficult for Captain Brown to get himself taken for what he really was. Few could seem to comprehend that freedom to the slaves was his only object. If you will go back with me to that time you will find that the most curious and contradictory versions of the affair were industriously circulated, and those which were the least rational and true seemed to command the readiest belief. In the view of some, it assumed tremendous proportions. To such it was nothing less than a wide-sweeping rebellion to overthrow the existing government, and construct another upon its ruins, with Brown for its President and Commander-in-Chief, the proof of this was found in the old man's carpet-bag in the shape of a constitution for a new Republic, an instrument which in reality had been executed to govern the conduct of his men in the mountains. Smaller and meaner natures saw in it nothing higher than a purpose to plunder. To them John Brown and his men were a gang of desperate robbers, who had learned by some means that the government had sent a large sum of money to Harper's Ferry to pay off the workmen in its employ there, and they had gone thence to fill their pockets from this money. The fact is, that outside of a few friends, scattered in different parts of the country, and the slaveholders of Virginia, few persons understood the significance of the hour. That a man might do something very audacious and desperate for money, power or fame, was to the general apprehension quite possible, but, in face of plainly-written law, in face of constitutional guarantees protecting each State against domestic violence, in face of a nation of forty million of people, that nineteen men could invade a great State to liberate a despised and hated race, was to the average intellect and conscience, too monstrous for belief. In this respect the vision of Virginia was clearer than that of the nation. Conscious of her guilt and therefore full of suspicion, sleeping on pistols for pillows, startled at every unusual sound, constantly fearing and expecting a repetition of the Nat Turner insurrection, she at once understood the meaning, if not the magnitude of the affair. It was this understanding which caused her to raise the lusty and imploring cry to the Federal government for help, and it was not till he who struck the blow had fully explained his motives and object, that the incredulous nation in any wise comprehended the true spirit of the raid, or of its commander. Fortunate for his memory, fortunate for the brave men associated with him, fortunate for the truth of history, John Brown survived the saber gashes, bayonet wounds and bullet holes, and was able, though covered with blood, to tell his own story and make his own defense. Had he with all his men, as might have been the case, gone down in the shock of battle, the world would have had no true basis for its judgment, and one of the most heroic efforts ever witnessed in behalf of liberty would have been confounded with base and selfish purposes. When, like savages, the Wises, the Vallandinghams, the Washingtons, the Stuarts and others stood around the fallen and bleeding hero, and sought by torturing questions to wring from his supposed dying lips some word by which to soil the sublime undertaking, by implicating Gerrit Smith, Joshua R. Giddings, Dr. S. G. Howe, G. L. Steams, Edwin Morton, Frank Sanborn, and other prominent Anti-slavery men, the brave old man, not only avowed his object to be the emancipation of the slaves, but serenely and proudly announced himself as solely responsible for all that had happened. Though some thought of his own life might at such a moment have seemed natural and excusable, he showed none, and scornfully rejected the idea that he acted as the agent or instrument of any man or set of men. He admitted that he had friends and sympathizers, but to his own head he invited all the bolts of slaveholding wrath and fury, and welcomed them to do their worst. His manly courage and self-forgetful nobleness were not lost upon the crowd about him, nor upon the country. They drew applause from his bitterest enemies. Said Henry A. Wise, "He is the gamest man I ever met." "He was kind and humane to his prisoners," said Col. Lewis Washington.

To the outward eye of men, John Brown was a criminal, but to their inward eye he was a just man and true. His deeds might be disowned, but the spirit which made those deeds possible was worthy highest honor. It has been often asked, why did not Virginia spare the life of this man? why did she not avail herself of this grand opportunity to add to her other glory that of a lofty magnanimity? Had they spared the good old man's life—had they said to him, "You see we have you in our power, and could easily take your life, but we have no desire to hurt you in any way; you have committed a terrible crime against society; you have invaded us at midnight and attacked a sleeping community, but we recognize you as a fanatic, and in some sense instigated by others; and on this ground and others, we release you. Go about your business, and tell those who sent you that we can afford to be magnanimous to our enemies." I say, had Virginia held some such language as this to John Brown, she would have inflicted a heavy blow on the whole Northern abolition movement, one which only the omnipotence of truth and the force of truth could have overcome. I have no doubt Gov. Wise would have done so gladly, but, alas, he was the executive of a State which thought she could not afford such magnanimity. She had that within her bosom which could more safely tolerate the presence of a criminal than a saint, a highway robber than a moral hero. All her hills and valleys were studded with material for a disastrous conflagration, and one spark of the dauntless spirit of Brown might set the whole State in flames. A sense of this appalling liability put an end to every noble consideration. His death was a foregone conclusion, and his trial was simply one of form.

Honor to the brave young Col. Hoyt who hastened from Massachusetts to defend his friend's life at the peril of his own; but there would have been no hope of success had he been allowed to plead the case. He might have surpassed Choate or Webster in power—a thousand physicians might have sworn that Capt. Brown was insane, it would have been all to no purpose, neither eloquence nor testimony could have prevailed. Slavery was the idol of Virginia, and pardon and life to Brown meant condemnation and death to slavery. He had practically illustrated a truth stranger than fiction,—a truth higher than Virginia had ever known,—a truth more noble and beautiful than Jefferson ever wrote. He had evinced a conception of the sacredness and value of liberty which transcended in sublimity that of her own Patrick Henry and made even his fire-flashing sentiment of "Liberty or Death" seem dark and tame and selfish. Henry loved liberty for himself, but this man loved liberty for all men, and for those most despised and scorned, as well as for those most esteemed and honored. Just here was the true glory of John Brown's mission. It was not for his own freedom that he was thus ready to lay down his life, for with Paul he could say, "I was born free." No chain had bound his ankle, no yoke had galled his neck. History has no better illustration of pure, disinterested benevolence. It was not Caucasian for Caucasian—white man for white man; not rich man for rich man, but Caucasian for Ethiopian—white man for black man—rich man for poor man—the man admitted and respected, for the man despised and rejected. "I want you to understand, gentlemen," he said to his persecutors, "that I respect the rights of the poorest and weakest of the colored people, oppressed by the slave system, as I do those of the most wealthy and powerful." In this we have the key to the whole life and career of the man. Than in this sentiment humanity has nothing more touching, reason nothing more noble, imagination nothing more sublime, and if we could reduce all the religions of the world to one essence we could find in it nothing more divine. It is much to be regretted that some great artist, in sympathy with the spirit of the occasion, had not been present when these and similar words were spoken. The situation was thrilling. An old man in the center of an excited and angry crowd, far away from home, in an enemy's country—with no friend near—overpowered, defeated, wounded, bleeding—covered with reproaches—his brave companions nearly all dead—his two faithful sons stark and cold by his side—reading his death-warrant in his fast-oozing blood and increasing weakness as in the faces of all around him—yet calm, collected, brave, with a heart for any fate—using his supposed dying moments to explain his course and vindicate his cause: such a subject would have been at once an inspiration and a power for one of the grandest historical pictures ever painted.

With John Brown, as with every other man fit to die for a cause, the hour of his physical weakness was the hour of his moral strength—the hour of his defeat was the hour of his triumph—the moment of his capture was the crowning victory of his life. With the Alleghany mountains for his pulpit, the country for his church and the whole civilized world for his audience, he was a thousand times more effective as a preacher than as a warrior, and the consciousness of this fact was the secret of his amazing complacency. Mighty with the sword of steel, he was mightier with the sword of the truth, and with this sword he literally swept the horizon. He was more than a match for all the Wises, Masons, Vallandighams and Washingtons, who could rise against him. They could kill him, but they could not answer him.

In studying the character and works of a great man, it is always desirable to learn in what he is distinguished from others, and what have been the causes of this difference. Such men as he whom we are now considering, come on to the theater of life only at long intervals. It is not always easy to explain the exact and logical causes that produce them, or the subtle influences which sustain them, at the immense heights where we sometimes find them, but we know that the hour and the man are seldom far apart, and that here, as elsewhere, the demand may in some mysterious way, regulate the supply. A great iniquity, hoary with age, proud and defiant, tainting the whole moral atmosphere of the country, subjecting both church and state to its control, demanded the startling shock which John Brown seemed especially inspired to give it.

Apart from this mission there was nothing very remarkable about him. He was a wool-dealer, and a good judge of wool, as a wool-dealer ought to be. In all visible respects he was a man like unto other men. No outward sign of Kansas or Harper's Ferry was about him. As I knew him, he was an even-tempered man, neither morose, malicious nor misanthropic, but kind, amiable, courteous, and gentle in his intercourse with men. His words were few, well chosen and forcible. He was a good business man, and a good neighbor. A good friend, a good citizen, a good husband and father: a man apparently in every way calculated to make a smooth and pleasant path for himself through the world. He loved society, he loved little children, he liked music, and was fond of animals. To no one was the world more beautiful or life more sweet. How then as I have said shall we explain his apparent indifference to life? I can find but one answer, and that is, his intense hatred to oppression. I have talked with many men, but I remember none, who seemed so deeply excited upon the subject of slavery as he. He would walk the room in agitation at mention of the word. He saw the evil through no mist or haze, but in a light of infinite brightness, which left no line of its ten thousand horrors out of sight. Law, religion, learning, were interposed in its behalf in vain. His law in regard to it was that which Lord Brougham described, as "the law above all the enactments of human codes, the same in all time, the same throughout the world—the law unchangeable and eternal—the law written by the finger of God on the human heart—that law by which property in man is, and ever must remain, a wild and guilty phantasy."

Against truth and right, legislative enactments were to his mind mere cobwebs—the pompous emptiness of human pride—the pitiful outbreathings of human nothingness. He used to say "whenever there is a right thing to be done, there is a ''thus saith the Lord' that it shall be done."

It must be admitted that Brown assumed tremendous responsibility in making war upon the peaceful people of Harper's Ferry, but it must be remembered also that in his eye a slaveholding community could not be peaceable, but was, in the nature of the case, in one incessant state of war. To him such a community was not more sacred than a band of robbers: it was the right of any one to assault it by day or night. He saw no hope that slavery would ever be abolished by moral or political means: "he knew," he said, "the proud and hard hearts of the slaveholders, and that they never would consent to give up their slaves, till they felt a big stick about their heads." It was five years before this event at Harper's Ferry, while the conflict between freedom and slavery was waxing hotter and hotter with every hour, that the blundering statesmanship of the National Government repealed the Missouri compromise, and thus launched the territory of Kansas as a prize to be battled for between the North and the South. The remarkable part taken in this contest by Brown has been already referred to, and it doubtless helped to prepare him for the final tragedy, and though it did not by any means originate the plan, it confirmed him in it and hastened its execution.

During his four years' service in Kansas it was my good fortune to see him often. On his trips to and from the territory he sometimes stopped several days at my house, and at one time several weeks. It was on this last occasion that liberty had been victorious in Kansas, and he felt that he must hereafter devote himself to what he considered his larger work. It was the theme of all his conversation, filling his nights with dreams and his days with visions. An incident of his boyhood may explain, in some measure, the intense abhorrence he felt to slavery. He had for some reason been sent into the State of Kentucky, where he made the acquaintance of a slave boy, about his own age, of whom he became very fond. For some petty offense this boy was one day subjected to a brutal beating. The blows were dealt with an iron shovel and fell fast and furiously upon his slender body. Born in a free State and unaccustomed to such scenes of cruelty, young Brown's pure and sensitive soul revolted at the shocking spectacle and at that early age he swore eternal hatred to slavery. After years never obliterated the impression, and he found in this early experience an argument against contempt for small things. It is true that the boy is the father of the man. From the acorn comes the oak. The impression of a horse's foot in the sand suggested the art of printing. The fall of an apple intimated the law of gravitation. A word dropped in the woods of Vincennes, by royal hunters, gave Europe and the world a "William the Silent," and a thirty years' war. The beating of a Hebrew bondsman, by an Egyptian, created a Moses, and the infliction of a similar outrage on a helpless slave boy in our own land may have caused, forty years afterwards, a John Brown and a Harper's Ferry Raid.

Most of us can remember some event or incident which has at some time come to us, and made itself a permanent part of our lives. Such an incident came to me in the year 1847. I had then the honor of spending a day and a night under the roof of a man, whose character and conversation made a very deep impression on my mind and heart; and as the circumstance does not lie entirely out of the range of our present observations, you will pardon for a moment a seeming digression. The name of the person alluded to had been several times mentioned to me, in a tone that made me curious to see him and to make his acquaintance. He was a merchant, and our first meeting was at his store—a substantial brick building, giving evidence of a flourishing business. After a few minutes' detention here, long enough for me to observe the neatness and order of the place, I was conducted by him to his residence where I was kindly received by his family as an expected guest. I was a little disappointed at the appearance of this man's house, for after seeing his fine store, I was prepared to see a fine residence; but this logic was entirely contradicted by the facts. The house was a small, wooden one, on a back street in a neighborhood of laboring men and mechanics, respectable enough, but not just the spot where one would expect to find the home of a successful merchant. Plain as was the outside, the inside was plainer. Its furniture might have pleased a Spartan. It would take longer to tell what was not in it, than what was, no sofas, no cushions, no curtains, no carpets, no easy rocking chairs inviting to enervation or rest or repose. My first meal passed under the misnomer of tea. It was none of your tea and toast sort, but potatoes and cabbage, and beef soup, such a meal as a man might relish after following the plough all day, or after performing a forced march of a dozen miles over rough ground in frosty weather. Innocent of paint, veneering, varnish or tablecloth, the table announced itself unmistakably and honestly pine and of the plainest workmanship. No hired help passed from kitchen to dining room, staring in amazement at the colored man at the white man's table. The mother, daughters and sons did the serving, and did it well. I heard no apology for doing their own work; they went through it as if used to it, untouched by any thought of degradation or impropriety. Supper over, the boys helped to clear the table and wash the dishes. This style of housekeeping struck me as a little odd. I mention it because household management is worthy of thought. A house is more than brick and mortar, wood or paint, this to me at least was. In its plainness it was a truthful reflection of its inmates: no disguises, no illusions, no make-believes here, but stern truth and solid purpose breathed in all its arrangements. I was not long in company with the master of this house before I discovered that he was indeed the master of it, and likely to become mine too, if I staid long with him. He fulfilled St. Paul's idea of the head of the family— his wife believed in him, and his children observed him with reverence. Whenever he spoke, his words commanded earnest attention. His arguments which I ventured at some points to oppose, seemed to convince all, his appeals touched all, and his will impressed all. Certainly I never felt myself in the presence of a stronger religious influence than while in this house. "God and duty, God and duty," run like a thread of gold through all his utterances, and his family supplied a ready "Amen." In person he was lean and sinewy, of the best New England mould, built for times of trouble, fitted to grapple with the flintiest hardships. Clad in plain American woolen, shod in boots of cowhide leather, and wearing a cravat of the same substantial material, under six feet high, less than one hundred and fifty lbs. in weight, aged about fifty, he presented a figure straight and symmetrical as a mountain pine. His bearing was singularly impressive. His head was not large, but compact and high. His hair was coarse, strong, slightly gray and closely trimmed and grew close to his forehead. His face was smoothly shaved and revealed a strong square mouth, supported by a broad and prominent chin. His eyes were clear and grey, and in conversation they alternated with tears and fire. When on the street, he moved with a long springing, race-horse step, absorbed by his own reflections, neither seeking nor shunning observation. Such was the man whose name I heard uttered in whispers—such was the house in which he lived—such were his family and household management—and such was Captain John Brown. He said to me at this meeting, that he had invited me to his house for the especial purpose of laying before me his plan for the speedy emancipation of my race. He seemed to apprehend opposition on my part as he opened the subject and touched my vanity by saying, that he had observed my course at home and abroad, and wanted my cooperation. He said he had been for the last thirty years looking for colored men to whom he could safely reveal his secret, and had almost despaired, at times, of finding such, but that now he was encouraged for he saw heads rising up in all directions, to whom he thought he could with safety impart his plan. As this plan then lay in his mind it was very simple, and had much to commend it. It did not, as was supposed by many, contemplate a general rising among the slaves, and a general slaughter of the slave masters (an insurrection he thought would only defeat the object), but it did contemplate the creating of an armed force which should act in the very heart of the South. He was not averse to the shedding of blood, and thought the practice of carrying arms would be a good one for the colored people to adopt, as it would give them a sense of manhood. No people he said could have self-respect or be respected who would not fight for their freedom. He called my attention to a large map of the U. States, and pointed out to me the far-reaching Alleghenies, stretching away from the borders of New York into the Southern States. "These mountains," he said, "are the basis of my plan. God has given the strength of these hills to freedom, they were placed here to aid the emancipation of your race; they are full of natural forts, where one man for defense would be equal to a hundred for attack; they are also full of good hiding places where a large number of men could be concealed and baffle and elude pursuit for a long time. I know these mountains well and could take a body of men into them and keep them there in spite of all the efforts of Virginia to dislodge me, and drive me out. I would take at first about twenty-five picked men and begin on a small scale, supply them arms and ammunition, post them in squads of fives on a line of twenty-five miles, these squads to busy themselves for a time in gathering recruits from the surrounding farms, seeking and selecting the most restless and daring." He saw that in this part of the work the utmost care must be used to guard against treachery and disclosure; only the most conscientious and skillful should be sent on this perilous duty. With care and enterprise he thought he could soon gather a force of one hundred hardy men, men who would be content to lead the free and adventurous life to which he proposed to train them. When once properly drilled and each had found the place for which he was best suited, they would begin work in earnest; they would run off the slaves in large numbers, retain the strong and brave ones in the mountains, and send the weak and timid ones to the North by the underground railroad, his operations would be enlarged with increasing numbers and would not be confined to one locality. Slaveholders should in some cases be approached at midnight and told to give up their slaves and to let them have their best horses to ride away upon. Slavery was a state of war, he said, to which the slaves were unwilling parties and consequently they had a right to anything necessary to their peace and freedom. He would shed no blood and would avoid a fight except in self-defense, when he would of course do his best. He believed this movement would weaken slavery in two ways—first by making slave property insecure, it would become undesirable; and secondly it would keep the anti-slavery agitation alive and public attention fixed upon it, and thus lead to the adoption of measures to abolish the evil altogether. He held that there was need of something startling to prevent the agitation of the question from dying out; that slavery had come near being abolished in Virginia by the Nat Turner insurrection, and he thought his method would speedily put an end to it, both in Maryland and Virginia. The trouble was to get the right men to start with and money enough to equip them. He had adopted the simple and economical mode of living to which I have referred with a view to save money for this purpose. This was said in no boastful tone, for he felt that he had delayed already too long and had no room to boast either his zeal or his self-denial.

From 8 o'clock in the evening till 3 in the morning, Capt. Brown and I sat face to face, he arguing in favor of his plan, and I finding all the objections I could against it. Now mark! this meeting of ours was full twelve years before the strike at Harper's Ferry. He had been watching and waiting all that time for suitable heads to rise or "pop up" as he said among the sable millions in whom he could confide; hence forty years had passed between his thought and his act. Forty years, though not a long time in the life of a nation, is a long time in the life of a man; and here forty long years, this man was struggling with this one idea; like Moses he was forty years in the wilderness. Youth, manhood, middle age had come and gone; two marriages had been consummated, twenty children had called him father; and through all the storms and vicissitudes of busy life, this one thought, like the angel in the burning bush, had confronted him with its blazing light, bidding him on to his work. Like Moses he had made excuses, and as with Moses his excuses were overruled. Nothing should postpone further what was to him a divine command, the performance of which seemed to him his only apology for existence. He often said to me, though life was sweet to him, he would willingly lay it down for the freedom of my people; and on one occasion he added, that he had already lived about as long as most men, since he had slept less, and if he should now lay down his life the loss would not be great, for in fact he knew no better use for it. During his last visit to us in Rochester there appeared in the newspapers a touching story connected with the horrors of the Sepoy War in British India. A Scotch missionary and his family were in the hands of the enemy, and were to be massacred the next morning. During the night, when they had given up every hope of rescue, suddenly the wife insisted that relief would come. Placing her ear close to the ground she declared she heard the Slogan—the Scotch war song. For long hours in the night no member of the family could hear the advancing music but herself. "Dinna ye hear it? Dinna ye hear it?" she would say, but they could not hear it. As the morning slowly dawned a Scotch regiment was found encamped indeed about them, and they were saved from the threatened slaughter. This circumstance, coming at such a time, gave Capt. Brown a new word of cheer. He would come to the table in the morning his countenance fairly illuminated, saying that he had heard the Slogan, and he would add, "Dinna ye hear it? Dinna ye hear it?" Alas! like the Scotch missionary I was obliged to say "No." Two weeks prior to the meditated attack, Capt. Brown summoned me to meet him in an old stone quarry on the Conecochequi river, near the town of Chambersburgh, Penn. His arms and ammunition were stored in that town and were to be moved on to Harper's Ferry. In company with Shields Green I obeyed the summons, and prompt to the hour we met the dear old man, with Kagi, his secretary, at the appointed place. Our meeting was in some sense a council of war. We spent the Saturday and succeeding Sunday in conference on the question, whether the desperate step should then be taken, or the old plan as already described should be carried out. He was for boldly striking Harper's Ferry at once and running the risk of getting into the mountains afterwards. I was for avoiding Harper's Ferry altogether. Shields Green and Mr. Kagi remained silent listeners throughout. It is needless to repeat here what was said, after what has happened. Suffice it, that after all I could say, I saw that my old friend had resolved on his course and that it was idle to parley. I told him finally that it was impossible for me to join him. I could see Harper's Ferry only as a trap of steel, and ourselves in the wrong side of it. He regretted my decision and we parted.

Thus far, I have spoken exclusively of Capt. Brown. Let me say a word or two of his brave and devoted men, and first of Shields Green. He was a fugitive slave from Charleston, South Carolina, and had attested his love of liberty by escaping from slavery and making his way through many dangers to Rochester, where he had lived in my family, and where he met the man with whom he went to the scaffold. I said to him, as I was about to leave, "Now Shields, you have heard our discussion. If in view of it, you do not wish to stay, you have but to say so, and you can go back with me." He answered, "I b'l'eve I'll go wid de old man;" and go with him he did, into the fight, and to the gallows, and bore himself as grandly as any of the number. At the moment when Capt. Brown was surrounded, and all chance of escape was cut off, Green was in the mountains and could have made his escape as Osborne Anderson did, but when asked to do so, he made the same answer he did at Chambersburg, "I b'l'eve I'll go down wid de ole man." When in prison at Charlestown, and he was not allowed to see his old friend, his fidelity to him was in no wise weakened, and no complaint against Brown could be extorted from him by those who talked with him.

If a monument should be erected to the memory of John Brown, as there ought to be, the form and name of Shields Green should have a conspicuous place upon it. It is a remarkable fact, that in this small company of men, but one showed any sign of weakness or regret for what he did or attempted to do. Poor Cook broke down and sought to save his life by representing that he had been deceived, and allured by false promises. But Stephens, Hazlett and Green went to their doom like the heroes they were, without a murmur, without a regret, believing alike in their captain and their cause.

For the disastrous termination of this invasion, several causes have been assigned. It has been said that Capt. Brown found it necessary to strike before he was ready; that men had promised to join him from the North who failed to arrive; that the cowardly Negroes did not rally to his support as he expected, but the true cause as stated by himself, contradicts all these theories, and from his statement there is no appeal. Among the questions put to him by Mr. Vallandingham after his capture were the following: "Did you expect a general uprising of the slaves in case of your success?" To this he answered, "No, sir, nor did

I wish it. I expected to gather strength from time to time and then to set them free." "Did you expect to hold possession here until then?" Answer, "Well, probably I had quite a different idea. I do not know as I ought to reveal my plans. I am here wounded and a prisoner because I foolishly permitted myself to be so. You overstate your strength when you suppose I could have been taken if I had not allowed it. I was too tardy after commencing the open attack in delaying my movements through Monday night and up to the time of the arrival of government troops. It was all because of my desire to spare the feelings of my prisoners and their families."

But the question is, Did John Brown fail? He certainly did fail to get out of Harper's Ferry before being beaten down by United States soldiers; he did fail to save his own life, and to lead a liberating army into the mountains of Virginia. But he did not go to Harper's Ferry to save his life. The true question is, Did John Brown draw his sword against slavery and thereby lose his life in vain? and to this I answer ten thousand times. No! No man fails, or can fail who so grandly gives himself and all he has to a righteous cause. No man, who in his hour of extremest need, when on his way to meet an ignominious death, could so forget himself as to stop and kiss a little child, one of the hated race for whom he was about to die, could by any possibility fail. Did John Brown fail? Ask Henry A. Wise in whose house less than two years after, a school for the emancipated slaves was taught. Did John Brown fail? Ask James M. Mason, the author of the inhuman fugitive slave bill, who was cooped up in Fort Warren, as a traitor less than two years from the time that he stood over the prostrate body of John Brown. Did John Brown fail? Ask Clement C. Vallandingham, one other of the inquisitorial party; for he too went down in the tremendous whirlpool created by the powerful hand of this bold invader. If John Brown did not end the war that ended slavery, he did at least begin the war that ended slavery. If we look over the dates, places and men, for which this honor is claimed, we shall find that not Carolina, but Virginia—not Fort Sumpter, but Harper's Ferry and the arsenal—not Col. Anderson, but John Brown, began the war that ended American slavery and made this a free Republic. Until this blow was struck, the prospect for freedom was dim, shadowy and uncertain. The irrepressible conflict was one of words, votes and compromises. When John Brown stretched forth his arm the sky was cleared. The time for compromises was gone—the armed hosts of freedom stood face to face over the chasm of a broken Union—and the clash of arms was at hand. The South staked all upon getting possession of the Federal Government, and failing to do that, drew the sword of rebellion and thus made her own, and not Brown's, the lost cause of the century.

The Race Problem
(1890)

This address serves primarily as Douglass's reaction to the attempts of southern Resurrectionists to limit African American's newly won civil rights, placing the responsibility of protecting those rights firmly in the hand of the federal government. It was delivered before the Bethel Literary and Historical Association on October 21, 1890, at the Metropolitan A.M.E. Church in Washington, D.C.

Members and Friends of the Bethel Literary and Historical Association.

I esteem it a great privilege to be with you and assist in this your first meeting since the close of your last winter's term. The organization of your association was an important step in the progress of the colored people in this city. It is an institution well fitted to improve the minds and elevate the sentiments not only of its members, but of the general public. Nowhere else outside of the courts of law and the Congress of the United States have I heard vital public questions more seriously discussed. The men selected to address you know very well that what they may utter is subjected to close scrutiny and severe discussion. Mere rant, bombast, and self-inflation may pass elsewhere, but not here. For this reason, and for my own self-respect, I shall endeavor to say only what I believe to be the truth upon what is popularly called "The Negro Problem."

My first thought respects the importance of calling things by their true names. This importance cannot be over-estimated or over-stated. Truth is the fundamental, indispensable, and everlasting requirement in obtaining right results. No department of human life can afford to dispense with truth. The carpenter cannot join his timbers without having the parts of contact perfectly true to each other. The mason cannot build a wall that will stand the test of time and gravitation without applying the plumb and making the wall vertical and true. No train or car is safe on the road where the relations of the rails are not true. No shot is certain of its aim where the gun-barrel is not true. As in mechanics, so in politics, morals, manners, metaphysics, and phi-

8

losophies, nothing can stand the test of time and experience that does not stand on the unassailable, indestructible, unchangeable, foundation of true. Considering how important this truth is, it seems strange that falsehood should hold such sway in the world. One main advantage by which error is able to darken, blight, and dominate the minds of men is the skill of its votaries in using language deceitfully, in pandering to prejudice by misstating and misapplying terms to the existing relations of men. It has been well said that in an important sense words are things. They are especially such when they are employed to express the popular sentiment concerning the Negro: to couple his name with anything in this world seems to damage it and damage him likewise. Hence I object to characterizing the relation subsisting between the white and colored people of this country as the Negro problem, as if the Negro had precipitated that problem, and as if he were in any way responsible for the problem. Though a rose by any other name may smell as sweet, it is not in good taste to give it a name that suggests offensive associations. There are, on the other hand, things that are in themselves revolting, and should not be given fair-seeming names. The slaveholders understood this principle well enough. Slavery lost something of its offensive aspect when it was called a domestic institution or a social system and other like names. Emancipation was made to look dangerous when it got itself called an experiment, although slavery itself was an experiment, and liberty is the normal condition of man. "The Negroes were the cause of the war," said Mr. Lincoln, and straightway the loyal soldiers of the Republic began to kick and beat the poor Negroes on the banks of the Potomac, and the Irish began to hang, stab, and murder the Negroes in New York. It is dangerous even to a dog to be given a bad name. I am, therefore, in favor of employing the truest and most agreeable names to describe the relation which at present subsists between ourselves and the other people of the country.

Again, another advantage to error, and one which is often employed with marked skill and effect, is the presentation to the minds of men of what may be called half truths for whole truths, and thus making a sweet and wholesome truth the cover for a bitter falsehood. A counterfeit nearest in likeness to what is genuine is always most likely to impose upon the unskillful. A lie ceases to be very dangerous when it parts with its ability to deceive. The devil is less dangerous as a roaring lion than when transformed as an angel of light.

The application of these homely truths and familiar examples will become apparent in the discussion I propose of what is popularly but improperly called the race problem. It seems that the American people have a special liking for this mathematical formula as applied to the Negro. They seem determined to keep his brain forever employed and his time forever occupied in solving a great variety of problems, and generally to his disadvantage. As soon as he solves one another is propounded to him, and when he thinks, good, easy soul, his work is done he finds a new one invented, a new burden imposed, and a new hardship inflicted. There may be rest for the weary, but there seems at present no rest for the Negro. He has been solving problems during all his history.

I have before referred in this place, I think, to the fact that the Negro was confronted 200 years ago by what was considered a great religious problem, one which was very difficult of solution. That problem was: Ought the Negro to be baptized in water and admitted to membership in the Christian church? This was, as I have often said, considering time of it, a tremendous problem. As in our day in regard to Negro problems, the opinions of the wise and great were strongly pronounced and much divided. The right of the Negro to baptism was fiercely disputed, especially by those who owned them as slaves. What is plain to all now was dark and doubtful to many then. It is easy to fancy that men spoke of it with bated breath, and saw in the Negro's baptism a menace to the peace and stability of society, as well as of slavery. For to baptize the Negro and admit him to membership in the Christian church was to recognize him as a man, a child of God, an heir of Heaven, redeemed by the blood of Christ, a temple of the Holy Ghost, a standing type and representative of the Savior of the world, one who, according to the apostle Paul, must be treated no longer as a servant, but as a brother beloved. Viewed in this light, his admission to baptism, and to the church was a matter for the gravest consideration. It touched the money nerve of the Christians of that day, for their wealth was largely invested in Negro flesh and blood. It was well said that the proposition was novel, extraordinary, and full of danger. It would impair the value of the slave, and it would put in jeopardy the authority of the master: they were right, and if the Negro is to be regarded as a Christian, he could not be regarded as a heathen, and as the Bible sanctioned only the enslavement of heathen, the Negro Christian could not be bought and sold, enslaved and, whipped, according to the requirements of the relation of master and slave. From every view they could then take of the proposition to baptize the Negro was rank radicalism and deserved stern resistance at its inception.

To the credit of the church and its ministers, it must be said that one learned and able divine, in the person of Dr. Godwin, was equal to the situation. He met the arguments of the opposition to Negro baptism in a book of 200 pages, in which he endeavored to show that baptism would not impair either the value of the slave or the authority of the master. His argument was a curious one. It divided the Negro into two separate parts, giving one to the Lord and the other to the slaveholder, and leaving nothing whatever of soul, body or spirit to himself. Baptism, he said, freed the Negro from the bondage of the devil, but not from the bondage of his earthly master. The controversy over this problem was long and furious, and the Negro only won a partial victory after all. The matter was finally settled, as usual, by a kind of compromise. The Negro was baptized and admitted to the church, but a sort of second table was set for him. He could take the Lord's supper only after his white brethren had finished eating the bread and drinking the wine. He was not even allowed to enter the same door of the sanctuary by which his white brethren entered. A separate door was cut for him in the wall, a sort of hole in the wall, leading to a high and dark place in the gallery, where his presence could give no offense to the Lord's white children on the floor.

It is strange that this state of things did not disgust and repel the Negro, make him an infidel, and drive him from religion altogether, but it did not. He clung to religion all the same. Believing that half a loaf was better than no bread, he took what he could get of the church, kept on praying and singing, and sometimes shouting. He could pray as fervently for the conversion of the scoundrel who tore his flesh with the lash, as for his best friend. He was made to think that his offensive black skin on earth would be changed for a white one in Heaven. It was a strange fancy, but quite a natural one when we see the importance given to color in the problems before us in our day.

Another problem greatly disturbed the conscientious during the time of slavery. It was this: Can a Negro contract a valid marriage? If he could, and could enforce his right to his wife and children, it would prove an inconvenient limitation on the power of his master. If what God has joined together no man shall put asunder, the right to sell the wife from the husband and the husband from the wife must cease. In the minds of the men who had to deal with it no such limitation in the right of the master could be allowed or tolerated for a moment. The master must have the right to buy and sell as he pleased, was the solution of that problem. One terrible evil of this solution of the marriage question is still seen in our land. Unable to contract valid marriage, the Negro felt himself unrestrained, and licensed to do as he pleased. He was not expected to limit his conduct by any rule or principle of morality or decency, but took to himself the freedom of the beasts of the field and the fowls of the air. He had in law no wife, no family, no children, and did not own himself. The consequence of this state of things may be seen very often in our own city at the police court and elsewhere, and the strange thing is, the very people who are responsible for this immorality and crime make merry over our wretchedness and talk solemnly about the terrible Negro problem.

Happily for us, and happily for our common country, as we shall see later on, the Southern solution of this Negro problem has now been unsolved by the act of emancipation and the superior civilization of the loyal American people over the people of the old slaveholding States.

Another troublesome problem presented to our Christian country was whether the Negro should have the help of the Bible with which to get to Heaven; whether, in fact, the command to search the Scriptures imposed any obligation or duty on him. Our Southern brethren, with whom we have always been profoundly sympathetic even unto this day, decided this problem against the Bible, and against the Negro, as usual. They made it a crime, to be punished with banishment, imprisonment, and stripes, for any one to teach the Negro to read. Yet the descendants of these same men, with the education of their fathers, and with the antecedents of their fathers, are now asking us in piteous tones to allow them in their superior wisdom and goodness of heart to solve what they are pleased to call the Negro problem of today. They are crying out lustily to the nation, like demons tormented before their time, "Hands off! We want no Federal authority, and want only local self-government. We want to be let alone!" They tell us that they know the Negro, and that they can manage him better than anybody else. They can manage his wages, his voting, and his education, and all that pertains to him. I hope the nation will not let them do any such thing. They have shown a strange inaptitude for such a task. The point with them is not what is right, but what will best suit themselves.

But again, in the history of the Negro we had another perplexing problem. It was this, and this was in some sense a national problem: Can the Negro be made a soldier? This, too, was very serious problem for the country, for it was a matter of Union or no Union, of life or death. For at one time it needed all the material which the nation could command to settle the problem of our national existence. It will be remembered that at the beginning of the war it was given out that no Negro need apply. He was not to be allowed to shoulder a musket, carry a knapsack, or wear a Union uniform. The glory of the battle-field was to be won wholly by white men. The Negro might dig but not fight. He might be a servant, but not a soldier. He might carry a pick-ax, but never a musket.

In considering this problem the nation, strangely enough, shut its eyes to the fact that in the history of the Revolution the Negro fought bravely for American independence, and in the war of 1812 he even extorted praise for his valor from the stern lips of General Andrew Jackson. His fighting qualities were nobly admitted by the hero of New Orleans. In spite of this it was insisted that the Negro was a born coward that could never make a soldier: that he would run at the sight of a gun. Time and events however helped the Negro and the Nation in the solution of this problem, as I think they will help in the solution of any others that may arise. Fort Wagner, Port Hudson, Vicksburg, James Island, Olustee, Petersburg, Richmond—a cloud of witnesses rise before us to solve the problem of the Negro's soldierly qualities.

Whether the Negro could be educated, was another problem, and I think this has been solved to the satisfaction of all candid men. He would be a dishonest man, or an amazingly stupid one who, in the face of the thousands of Negro teachers, the hundreds of Negro preachers, doctors, lawyers, authors, and editors, with which the country is now studded, should insist, as it was once insisted, that education was impossible to the Negro.

But the greatest problem for the Negro was whether he could with safety be made free. Good men knew that slavery was wrong, but how to get rid of it was the great question. Neither the pulpit, nor the press, nor the statesman could see a solution of the great problem, and yet that problem has been solved. The Negro is free, and the country is cleansed of its greatest curse, crime, and scandal.

There were terrible things to happen upon the passing away of slavery. The freedom of the slave was the signal of ruin. There was to be no more cotton, no more sugar, no more work done by the Negro, and the South was to become a howling wilderness. But against all these dark forebodings, these pictures of dismal terror, the late was made short work of the whole problem. That sturdy old Roman, Benjamin Butler, made the Negro a contraband, Abraham Lincoln made him a free man, and General Ulysses S. Grant made him a citizen, and not one of these terrible things have happened.

But now, though all this has been done, though slavery has been abolished, though the Negro has been freed, though he has become a citizen, though the Union has been saved, in part by his valor, the Negro is not to be let off quite yet. He is to be made the victim of a new deal by precipitating upon the country a false issue. He is to face another problem.

Now that the Union is no longer in danger, now that the North and South are no longer enemies: now that they have ceased to scatter, tear, and slay each other, but sit together in halls of Congress, commerce, religion, and in brotherly love, it seems that the Negro is to lose by their sectional harmony and good will all the rights and privileges that he gained by their former bitter enmity.

This, it is found, cannot be accomplished without confusing the moral sense of the nation and misleading the public mind; without creating doubt, inflaming passion, arousing prejudice, and attracting to the enemies of the Negro the popular sympathy by representing the Negro as an ignorant, base, and dangerous person, and by presenting to those enemies that his existence to them is a dreadful problem. With their usual cunning, these enemies of the Negro have made the North partly believe that they are now contending with a vast and mysterious problem, the mere contemplation of which should cause the whole North to shudder and come to the rescue. The trick is worthy of its inventors, and has been played for all that it is worth. The orators of the South have gone North and have eloquently described this terrible problem, and the press of the South has flamed with it, and grave Senators from that section have painted it in most distressing colors. Problem, problem, race problem, Negro problem, has, as Junius says, fitted through their sentences in all the mazes of metaphorical confusion.

In speaking of this subject in another place, I said what I say now, that these Southern people have outwitted the North in this problem business. Like skillful prestidigitators, they have turned the attention of the spectator to a distant object while they have manipulated the thing in hand. They imitated the cunning of the hunter who draws a red herring across the path of the game to divert the hounds.

The true problem is not the Negro, but the nation. Not the law-abiding blacks of the South, but the white men of that section, who by fraud, violence, and persecution, are breaking the law, trampling on the Constitution, corrupting the ballot-box, and defeating the ends of justice. The true problem is whether these white ruffians shall be allowed by the nation to go on in their lawless and nefarious career, dishonoring the Government and making its very name a mockery. It is whether this nation has in itself sufficient moral stamina to maintain its own honor and integrity by vindicating its own Constitution and fulfilling its own pledges, or whether it has already touched that dry rot of moral depravity by which nations decline and fall, and governments fade and vanish. The United States Government made the Negro a citizen; will it protect him as a citizen? This is the problem. It made him a soldier; will it honor him as a patriot? This is the problem. It made him a voter; will it defend his right to vote? This is the problem. This, I say, is more a problem for the nation than for the Negro, and this is the side of the question far more than the other, which should be kept in view by the American people.

What these problem orators now ask is that the nation shall undo all that it did by the suppression of the rebellion and in maintenance of the Union. They ask that the nation shall recede from its advance in the path of justice, liberty, and civilization. They boldly ask that what was justly and gratefully given to the Negro in the hour of national peril shall be taken from him in the hour of national security. They ask that the nation shall stultify itself and commit an act of national shame which ought to make every lover of his country cry out in bitter indignation and unite as one man to oppose. A demand so scandalous and so shocking to every sentiment of honor and gratitude.

And from whom does this demand come? Not from who gave their lives to save the nation, but from those who gave their lives to destroy it. Not from the free and loyal North, but from the rebellious and slaveholding South. Not from the section where men go to the ballot-box with the same freedom from personal danger as they go to church on Sunday, but from that section where personal safety is endangered, where Federal authority is defied, where the amendments to the Constitution are nullified, where the ballot-box is tainted by fraud, and red-shirted intimidation makes a free vote impossible. It comes from the men who led the nation in a dance of blood during four long years, and who now have the impudence to assume to control the destiny of this Republic as well as the destiny of the Negro.

And what are the reasons they give for demanding of the nation this retreat from its advanced position? They are these: They tell us that they are afraid, very much afraid: they are alarmed, very much alarmed, by the possibility of Negro supremacy over them. This is the calamity from which they would be delivered, and with eloquent lips and lusty lungs they are calling out: "Men and brethren, save us from this threatened and terrible danger!" My reply to this alarm is easy. It is that the wicked flee when no man pursueth: that the thief thinks each bush an officer: that the thing they pretend to fear can never happen, and that blank absurdity is written upon the face of it. The eagle, with fierce talon and bloody beak screaming in terror at the approach of a harmless black bird would not be more absurd and ridiculous. The superior intelligence of the whites, the comparative ignorance of the blacks, the former dominion of the whites and the former subjection of the blacks, the habit of bearing rule of the whites, and the habit of submission by the blacks make black supremacy in any part of our common country utterly impossible.

But supposing such an occurrence possible, what hardship would it impose? What wrong would it inflict? Who would be injured by it? If the blacks should get the upper hand, their rule would have to be regulated by the Constitution and the laws of the United States. They could not discriminate against white people on account of race, color, or previous condition without findings the iron hand of the nation laid heavily on their shoulders. The white people of the South are

the rich, the Negroes the poor; the white people are the landown-
ers, the Negroes are the landlers. The white people of the South are
numbered with the ruling class of the nation. They have behind them
every possible source of power. They have railroads, steamships, electric
telegraphs, the Army and the Navy. They have the sword and the purse
of the nation behind them, and yet they profess to be shaking in their
shoes lest the 8,000,000 of blacks shall come to rule over them and
their brethren, the 50,000,000 of whites.

Now I am here to say that there is nothing whatever in this supposi-
tion. I can hardly call this invention a cunning device, for the pretense
is too open, too transparent, too absurd, to rise even to the dignity of
low cunning. It is an old ragged pair of trousers, and an old mashed
and battered hat of the last century stuck upon a pole in a field where
there are neither crows nor corn. It is the cry of fire by the thief when
he would divert the officer of the law. It is as I have said, a red herring
to divert the hounds from the true game, and the strange thing is that
any class of our citizens, white or black, can be deceived by it.

But black supremacy is not the only string on the harp of a thousand strings upon which our Southern brethren play. They are not
merely afraid of black supremacy, but they are afraid of ignorant black
supremacy. Now, this danger is just the one to appeal to the sympathy
of the North. The Northern people are not in love with ignorance
or illiteracy. They deplore it; they hate it, and take every means in
their power to banish it from their States. They naturally sympathize
with any people in deploring it and who are making honest efforts to
remove it from among them. Hence they are pouring out millions of
dollars to aid the South, and are sending competent teachers there to
enlighten the ignorant and to lift up the black man and white man alike
from the darkness and ignorance to which they had been doomed by
slavery and by those would-be Negro problem solvers.

But it is worthy of emphatic remark that the men in the South who
are loudest in their outcry against the ignorance of the Negro are not
those who wish to have him instructed, but those who would make
his ignorance a reason for depriving him of the rights secured to him
under the Constitution.

But again, when before in the history of the Southern people have
they been alarmed by the presence of ignorance among them? When
before did they ask the nation to assist them in stemming the tide of
ignorance? The whole history of the legislation of the South—by the
South I mean the ruling class of the South—is on the side of ignorance. Their laws have made it a crime to enlighten the black man's
ignorance. It has been the policy of the ruling class there to oppose
education not only for the blacks, but for the poor whites as well. But

as I have said, this cry is raised not for help to educate the Negro, but as an excuse for taking from him the right of suffrage, by which he can in some measure promote his own education and the education of those about him.

But admitting what I do not admit, that the ignorance of the Negro is recognized by the South as a source of danger, and admitting the sincerity of Southern men who are professing to deplore it, I have to say to them: If you could stand the Negro when he was a slave, you can stand it now that he is free, at least a reasonable length of time for his education. Clearly enough, the remedy is not in the abridgement of his rights, but in the education of his mind. It is not in evading the plain provisions of the Constitution, but in teaching him the duties imposed by the Constitution; not in taking away his vote, but in teaching him how to use it.

To me there is something very audacious and insolent rather than pathetic and persuasive in the language employed by Southern men on this question. There is something of the old-time Southern swagger and assumption in their tone and bearing—a tone and bearing which is entirely out of date, out of place, and out of harmony with the age body of our time—a tone and bearing which invites rebuke rather than sympathy, disgust rather than approbation.

Such men as Senator Butler, of South Carolina, should remember that there is such a thing as modesty as well as decency for men of such antecedents as theirs and that it is neither modest nor decent for them to coolly propose the expulsion of citizen innocent of crime from the State of South Carolina, or from any other State in the American Union. It is only a little while ago that Senator Butler and his class were in arms against the Government which these same Negro citizens loyally and bravely endeavored to save from their disloyal hands.

But let me say again, the South neither really fears the ignorance of the Negro, nor the supremacy of the Negro. It is not the ignorant Negro, but the intelligent North that it fears; not the supremacy of a different race from itself, but the supremacy of the Republican Party. It is not the men who are emancipated but the people who emancipated them that disturb its repose. In other words the trouble is not racial, but political. It is not the race and color of the vote. Disguise this as it may, the real thing that troubles the South is the Republican party, its principles, and its ascendancy in Southern States and the nation. When it talks of Negro ignorance, Negro supremacy, it means this, and simply this, only this. It uses the word Negro simply as a means to the end of awakening popular prejudice and enlisting its influence in favor of its bad cause, a cause for which they have shown themselves capable of committing every description of frauds the most scandalous, and cruelty the most barbarous. We all know that the Negro problem would vanish into thin air, would utterly disappear like the mist before the morning sun, if the intelligent Negroes of the South would renounce their connection with the Republican Party and support only the Democratic party. What the South wants, and what it means to have peaceably if it can, or forcibly if it must, is a solid Democratic Party South and Democratic rule in the nation. There is not an intelligent man at the South that does not know this, and there is not an honest man at the South, who, if he would speak candidly on the subject, would deny this. The trouble is that the people of the North do not see this in its true light. Honest themselves, they cannot readily believe that others are not alike honest. It is in some sense creditable in them that they have never believed in the story of outrages committed against the Negro voters of the South, because they themselves would not be guilty of such outrages, they have been easily imposed upon by the pretended fear of a Negro supremacy professed by the South.

But let me be more intelligible. My idea about the problem business is this When a case has been in litigation before a court of highest resort, and that case has been solemnly adjudicated in that court, that case is finished and all the parties to it must submit to the decision or become law-breakers and criminals. The case goes into history hence forth *res adjudicata*. It is settled. If this beneficent rule did not exist there would be no end to litigation and no response for the public mind.

To make my meaning still more clear: When in England a few years ago Northampton saw it fit to send Mr. Bradlaugh, an infidel, to represent it in the British House of Commons, and he was not allowed to take his seat, the admission of an infidel to the House of Commons was a problem: but when he continued to knock at the door of the House till he was finally admitted the infidel problem, so far as the right of membership of that House was concerned, was solved.

Again, we are not the only people whose rights have been denied on the ground of race. Our brother Shem has had a taste of proscription as well as ourselves. No Jew was at one time eligible to membership in the parliament of Great Britain, but after long years of agitation of the question, Mr. Baring, an eminent Jew, was admitted to a seat in parliament. The Jewish problem, when Mr. Baring was seated, was ended, I mean this: When the American people declared their independence of Great Britain and made good that declaration by victory in a seven years war, the problem of American independence was solved, and there was never anything afterwards concerning it which could be called problematical. It was a fixed fact, and has remained such until now, and will remain so, I trust, forever.

There is a grand agitation now in progress in Great Britain for local self-government, at the head of which are Mr. Gladstone and Mr. Parnell. If Great Britain shall grant home rule to Ireland, the Irish problem will be solved, and it will be nonsense thereafter to speak of it as an unsolved problem. Our American women are asking for a sixteenth amendment to the Constitution, whereby they may vote. They ought to have it. If the American people shall adopt such an amendment, the women problem will cease to exist.

In like manner, when the Negro was declared free by the highest authority in the land, when the whole system of his bondage was broken up, when he was invested by the organic law of the land with the title, dignity and immunity of an American citizen, and when it was declared that any discrimination made by any State against him on account of race or color was unlawful, I hold that his race condition could no longer be consider a problem. The thing was done: it was finished. The nation had taken its position and all the parts of the nation must ultimately adjust themselves to the whole. The individual States may be great, but the United States is greater. The mountain will not and cannot go to Mahomet, so Mahomet must and will in the end go to the mountain. Herein is the ground of my hope.

The trend of civilization, the power of large bodies to attract small ones, the force of national greatness, the inclination to the stronger rather than to the weak in human forces will ultimately bring the individual States in line with the Federal body. I affirm that while the National Government shall remain in the hands of the Republican party and under the principles of that party, no State will or can permanently disenfranchise any of its citizens because of race or color or previous condition. Attempts may be made to do this, but the race problem in that respect is solved, and the case cannot be permanently reopened.

But I am asked, what of the future? and will the various peoples of this country ever be thoroughly assimilated? or, to speak more plainly, will they ever intermarry? My answer is, "Sufficient unto the day is the evil thereof." We should not cross the stream till we have come to it. Whether such marriages will ever become common or not is no matter of vital concern to anybody at this day. It is mere speculation and is utterly without practical importance, so far as the rights of the American people are concerned. It touches no question of politics, statesmanship, or religion.

Individual interests, personal preferences and public sentiment may be safely left to regulate the relations of the races in respect of intermarriage. Such, I think, is the view that common sense will take of it, but such does not seem to be the view taken of it by some of our people—white, black and mixed. There seems to be a fascination about the subject which makes it impossible for men to let alone. They thrust it into our faces on all occasions, in season and out of season, and seem distressed because we cannot solve the problem for them. Some of them say that the repugnance of the white race of the black makes marriages between them impossible, and yet they proceed with great warmth and eloquence to denounce it as a thing to be closely watched and guarded against, and by no means encouraged. If the thing is impossible to happen no one should be afraid that it will happen.

I noticed while at my post in Haiti that even the Senate of the United States was compelled to listen to a learned disquisition upon this subject of race intermarriage from the lips of the eloquent, learned, and distinguished Senator from Kansas. I have always entertained for that gifted gentleman the highest respect. When he is right he is very right and when he is wrong he is very wrong. There is no halfness is his character and composition. He is either all or he is nothing. In the present instance he happens to be not only all wrong, but very wrong. His argument against the admixture of the race is intense but narrow, brilliant but unsound, learned but inconsistent and illogical. He not only contradicts the facts and the science of the case but contradicts himself. He asserts that only the bad qualities of each race inherited by a mixed race, and at the same time he permits himself to say that he attributes whatever ability I happen to possess to the Caucasian side of my parentage. So good a logician as Senator Ingalls should not have allowed himself, almost in the same breath, to knock down the whole superstructure of his argument. Mr. Ingalls is a brave and a generous man, and I am surprised that these qualities were allowed to forsake him on the occasion referred to. Had he listened to the manly side of his character he would have never allowed himself to slay with his brilliant rhetoric a million of his colored fellow-citizens.

He took advantage of his position on the floor of the United States Senate to deal us a blow which we had no means of parrying. His advantage was great, and the ignoble character of his attack must be measured by the greatness of his advantage. Had any colored man of spirit and ability been a member of the Senate to reply to his assault. Mr. Ingalls would not have been inconsistent with his well-known chivalric qualities. But the case was otherwise.

If it be true that good qualities are not transmissible in such unions; if it be true that only evil, and that continually, must descend to the children of such parents, it may be well asked why any of the mulatto or quadroon children and grandchildren of our earlier statesmen are found anywhere outside of the thick walls and iron-barred windows of our prisons. Why are they walking our streets and employed in our houses as trusted servants and stewards? Why are they our teachers, professors, and preachers? Why are they respected and treated as gentlemen and Christians in every part of the world except our own? Oh, no, Mr. Ingalls! Your argument will not hold. It will not bear the test of either reason or experience.

Your language is the language of alarm, and the question you should put to yourself is. What if, in a nation of a hundred millions there should occasionally happen a marriage between two different varieties of the human family? Who would be hurt by it? Who, outside the parties themselves, should give themselves any trouble about it? The sun would not cease to shine, the rain to descend, nor the grass to grow. Men would not cease to go to and fro in the earth, or knowledge cease to roll onward. If the country has endured, during 240 years, lawless relations on a broad scale between the two peoples, it should not go into paroxysms of alarm over what may possibly take place under lawful conditions.

And now comes Mr. Isaiah Montgomery, of Mississippi, with his solution of the pretended Negro problem. I have spoken of him elsewhere, and I take back nothing that I have said either of this remarkable man, or his remarkable address. He has surrendered to a disloyal State a great franchise given to himself and his people by the loyal nation. He has taken the work of solving the nation's work of the nation's hands. He has virtually said to the nation:

"You have done wrong in giving us this great liberty. You should give us back a part of our bondage." He has surrendered a part of his rights to an enemy who will make this surrender a reason for demanding all of his rights. He has conducted his people to a depth from which they will be invited to a lower deep, for if he can rightfully surrender a part of his heritage from the National Government at the bidding of his oppressors, he may surrender the whole. The people with whom he makes this deal are restrained in dealing with the rights of colored men by no sense of modesty or moderation in their demands. They want all that is to be had, and will take all that they can get. Their real sentiment is that no Negro shall or ought to have the right to vote. Yet I have no denunciation for the man Montgomery. He is not a conscious traitor though his act is treason: treason to the cause of the colored people, not only of his own State, but of the United States.

I wish the consequences of his act could be confined to Mississippi alone, but I fear this cannot be. Other colored men in other States, dazzled by the fame obtained by Mr. Montgomery through the Democratic press, will probably imitate his bad example. I speak of this Montgomery business more in sorrow than in anger. I hear in the plaintive eloquence of his marvelous address a groan of bitter anguish born of oppression and despair. It is the voice of a soul from which all hope has vanished. His deed kindles indignation to be sure, but his condition awakens pity. He had called to the nation for help—help which it ought to have rendered and could have rendered but it did not—and in a moment of impatience and despair he has thought to make terms with the enemy, an enemy with whom no colored man can make terms but by a sacrifice of his manhood. There is no need here of an analysis of Mr. Montgomery's address. Its character is known and it has nothing to commend it but its ability and plaintive eloquence and the man, the place, and the circumstances under which it was delivered. The logic of the speech would have conducted magnanimous men to a prompt rejection of the surrender, for it was an appeal to all that was noble, grateful, and generous in hearts of Mississippians. They should have said, "No, Mr. Montgomery: your people have been our best friends when we needed friends, and we scorn to take from you the franchise accorded to you by the wisdom and magnanimity of the National Government."

Ladies and gentlemen: I have been requested to say an encouraging word to our people before I leave for my post of duty at Port-au-Prince, and if I have not already said such a word I find it quite easy to do so now. From every view I have been able to take of the moral and political situation of our cause, before and since my arrival in the country, I am hopeful. I have no doubt whatever of the future. I know that there are times in the history of all reforms when the future looks dark; when the friends of reform are impatient and despondent; when they cannot see the end from the beginning; when the truth that is plain to them compels them to reject the honesty of all who receive it. When they meet with opposition where they expected cooperation; when they met with treachery where they expected fidelity, and defeat where they expected victory. I, for one, have gone through all this. I have had fifty years of it, and yet I have not lost either heart or hope. It is true that we have been sadly disappointed in the action, or rather non-action, of the Fifty-first Congress. The platform of the Republican party adopted at Chicago plainly committed the Republican party to some measure of protection to the Republican voters of the South. We had right to expect the pledge there given would find fulfillment in the action of this Republican Congress. We have been disappointed, sadly disappointed. Following the advice of a new leader from Pennsylvania, but a leader not of the Thaddeus Stevens and Charles Sumner mold, this Congress has preferred protection to commerce and property to protection to personal and political liberty. We had hoped that it would adopt either the Federal election bill or the

Blair educational bill. It has done neither. The omission is, on the face of it, discouraging. But what then? Shall we get mad and denounce and renounce the Republican Party? Has that party sinned away its day of grace? Are there no remaining reasons for giving it our confidence? I entertain no such thought. The Federal election and educational bills are not dead, nor are their Senate; and the House may permit delay, but they will not suffer defeat. The president of the United States is true to his trust. No man since General Grant has stood by us more firmly than has General Harrison. He has let it be known openly and emphatically that he is for stepping to the very verge of constitutional limitations to secure honest elections, a free vote, and a fair count in every State in the Union, and he is not the man to take any steps backward.

I admit that during many years to come the colored man will have to endure prejudice against his race and color, but this constitutes no problem to vex and disturb the course of legislation. The world was never yet without prejudice. There exists prejudice in favor of and against classes among men of the same race and color. There is prejudice between religious sects and denominations; between Catholic and Protestant; between families and individuals. The time may never come this side the millennium when men will not ask "Can any good thing come out of Nazareth?" But what business has government, State or National, with these prejudices? Why should grave statesmen concern themselves with them? The business of government is to hold its broad shield over all and to see that every American citizen is alike and equally protected in his civil and personal rights. My confidence is strong and high in the nation as a whole. I believe in its justice and in its power. I believe that it means to keep its word with its colored citizens. I believe in its progress, in its moral as well as its material civilization. Its trend is in the right direction. Its fundamental principles are sound. Its conception of humanity and of human rights is clear and comprehensive. Its progress is fettered by no State religion tending to repress liberal thought: by no order of nobility tending to keep down the toiling masses: by no divine right theory tending to national stagnation under the idea of stability. It stands out free and clear with nothing to obstruct its view of the lessons of reason and experience.

It may be said, as has been said, that I am growing old, and am easily satisfied with things as they are. When our young men shall have worked and waited for victory as long as I have worked and waited, they will not only learn to have patience with the men opposed to them, but with me also for having patience with such. I have seen dark hours in my life, and I have seen the darkness gradually disappearing and the light gradually increasing. One by one I have seen obstacles removed, errors corrected, prejudices softened, proscriptions relinquished, and my people advancing in all the elements that go to make up the sum of general welfare. And I remember that God reigns in eternity, and that whatever delays, whatever disappointments and discouragements may come, truth, justice, liberty and humanity will ultimately prevail.

Lecture on Haiti
(1893)

Frederick Douglass served as the United States Ambassador to Haiti from 1889 to 1891. In the following address, delivered on January 2, 1893 at the Haitian Pavilion of the World's Fair in Chicago, Douglass speaks about Haiti's long road from a slave colony to a free state, and why African Americans should work to ensure a good relationship between the U.S. and Haiti.

No man should presume to come before an intelligent American audience without a commanding object and an earnest purpose. In whatever else I may be deficient, I hope I am qualified, both in object and purpose, to speak to you this evening.

My subject is Haiti, the Black Republic; the only self-made Black Republic in the world. I am to speak to you of her character, her history, her importance and her struggle from slavery to freedom and to statehood. I am to speak to you of her progress in the line of civilization; of her relation with the United States; of her past and present; of her probable destiny; and of the bearing of her example as a free and independent Republic, upon what may be the destiny of the African race in our own country and elsewhere.

If, by a true statement of facts and a fair deduction from them, I shall in any degree promote a better understanding of what Haiti is, and create a higher appreciation of her merits and services to the world; and especially, if I can promote a more friendly feeling for her in this country and at the same time give to Haiti herself a friendly hint as to what is hopefully and justly expected of her by her friends, and by the civilized world, my object and purpose will have been accomplished.

There are many reasons why a good understanding should exist between Haiti and the United States. Her proximity; her similar government and her large and increasing commerce with us, should alone make us deeply interested in her welfare, her history, her progress and her possible destiny.

Haiti is a rich country. She has many things which we need and we have many things which she needs. Intercourse between us is easy. Measuring distance by time and improved steam navigation, Haiti will one day be only three days from New York and thirty-six hours from Florida; in fact our next door neighbor. On this account, as well as others equally important, friendly and helpful relations should subsist between the two countries. Though we have a thousand years of civilization behind us, and Haiti only a century behind her; though we are large and Haiti is small; though we are strong and Haiti is weak; though we are a continent and Haiti is bounded on all sides by the sea, there may come a time when even in the weakness of Haiti there may be strength to the United States.

Now, notwithstanding this plain possibility, it is a remarkable and lamentable fact, that while Haiti is so near us and so capable of being so serviceable to us; while, like us, she is trying to be a sister republic and anxious to have a government of the people, by the people and for the people; while she is one of our very best customers, selling her coffee and her other valuable products to Europe for gold, and sending us her gold to buy our flour, our fish, our oil, our beef and our pork; while she is thus enriching our merchants and our farmers and our country generally, she is the one country to which we turn the cold shoulder.

We charge her with being more friendly to France and to other European countries than to ourselves. This charge, if true, has a natural explanation, and the fault is more with us than with Haiti. No man can point to any act of ours to win the respect and friendship of this black republic. If, as is alleged, Haiti is more cordial to France than to the United States, it is partly because Haiti is herself French. Her language is French; her literature is French, her manners and fashions are French; her ambitions and aspirations are French; her laws and methods of government are French; her priesthood and her education are French; her children are sent to school in France and their minds are filled with French ideas and French glory.

But a deeper reason for coolness between the countries is this: Haiti is black, and we have not yet forgiven Haiti for being black or forgiven the Almighty for making her black. In this enlightened act of repentance and forgiveness, our boasted civilization is far behind all other nations. In every other country on the globe a citizen of Haiti is sure of civil treatment. In every other nation his manhood is recognized and respected. Wherever any man can go, he can go. He is not repulsed, excluded or insulted because of his color. All places of amusement and instruction are open to him. Vastly different is the case with him when he ventures within the border of the United States. Besides, after Haiti had shaken off the fetters of bondage, and long after her freedom and independence had been recognized by all other civilized nations, we continued to refuse to acknowledge the fact and treated her as outside the sisterhood of nations.

No people would be likely soon to forget such treatment and fail to resent it in one form or another. Not to do so would justly invite contempt.

In the nature of the country itself there is much to inspire its people with manliness, courage and self-respect. In its typography it is wonderfully beautiful, grand and impressive. Clothed in its blue and balmy atmosphere it rises from the surrounding sea in surpassing splendor. In describing the grandeur and sublimity of this country, the Haitian may well enough adopt the poetic description of our own proud country:

A land of forests and of rock,
Of deep blue sea and mighty river,
Of mountains reared aloft to mock,
The thunder shock, the lightning's quiver;
My own green land forever.

It is a land strikingly beautiful, diversified by mountains, valleys, lakes, rivers and plains, and contains in itself all the elements of great and enduring wealth. Its limestone formation and foundation are a guarantee of perpetual fertility. Its tropical heat and insular moisture keep its vegetation fresh, green and vigorous all the year round. At an altitude of eight thousand feet, its mountains are still covered with woods of great variety and of great value. Its climate, varying with altitude like that of California, is adapted to all constitutions and productions.

Fortunate in its climate and soil, it is equally fortunate in its adaptation to commerce. Its shoreline is marked with numerous indentations of inlets, rivers, bays and harbors, where every grade of vessel may anchor in safety. Bulwarked on either side by lofty mountains rich with tropical verdure from base to summit, its blue waters dotted here and there with the white wings of commerce from every land and sea, the Bay of Port au Prince almost rivals the far-famed Bay of Naples, the most beautiful in the world.

One of these bays has attracted the eyes of American statesmanship. The Mole St. Nicolas of which we have heard much and may hear much more, is a splendid harbor. It is properly styled the Gibraltar of that country. It commands the Windward Passage, the natural gateway of the commerce both of the new and old world. Important now, our statesmanship sees that it will be still more important when the Nicaragua Canal shall be completed. Hence we want this harbor for a naval station. It is seen that the nation that can get it and hold it will be master of the land and sea in its neighborhood. Some rash things have been said by Americans about getting possession of this harbor. We are to have it peaceably, if we can, forcibly, if we must. I hardly think we shall get it by either process, for the reason that Haiti will not surrender peacefully, and it would cost altogether too much to wrest it from her by force. I thought in my simplicity when Minister and Council General to Haiti, that she might as an act of comity, make this concession to the United States, but I soon found that the judgment of the American Minister was not the judgment of Haiti. Until I made the effort to obtain it I did not know the strength and vigor of the sentiment by which it would be withheld. Haiti has no repugnance to losing control over a single inch of her territory. No statesman in Haiti would dare to disregard this sentiment. It could not be done by any government without costing the country revolution and bloodshed. I did not believe that President Harrison wished me to press the matter to any such issue. On the contrary, I believe as a friend to the colored race he desired peace in that country.

The attempt to create angry feeling in the United States against Haiti because she thought proper to refuse us the Mole St. Nicolas, is neither reasonable nor creditable. There was no insult or broken faith in the case. Haiti has the same right to refuse that we had to ask, and there was insult neither in the asking nor in the refusal.

Neither the commercial, geographical or numerical importance of Haiti is to be despised. If she wants much from the world, the world wants much that she possesses. She produces coffee, cotton, log-wood, mahogany and lignum-vitae. The revenue realized by the government from these products is between nine and ten millions of dollars. With such an income, if Haiti could be kept free from revolutions, she might easily become, in proportion to her territory and population, the richest country in the world. And yet she is comparatively poor, not because she is revolutionary.

The population of Haiti is estimated to be nearly one million. I think the actual number exceeds this estimate. In the towns and cities of the country the people are largely of mixed blood and range all the way from black to white. But the people of the interior are of pure Negro blood. The prevailing color among them is a dark brown with a dash of chocolate in it. They are in many respects a fine looking people. There is about them a sort of majesty. They carry themselves proudly erect as if conscious of their freedom and independence. I thought the women quite superior to the men. They are elastic, vigorous and comely. They move with the step of a blooded horse. The industry, wealth and prosperity of the country depends largely upon them. They supply the towns and cities of Haiti with provisions, bringing them from distances of fifteen and twenty miles, and they often bear an additional burden in the shape of a baby. This baby burden is curiously tied to the sides of the mother. They seem to think nothing of their burden, the length of the journey or the added weight of the baby. Thousands of these country women in their plain blue gowns and many colored turbans, every morning line the roads leading into Port au Prince. The spectacle is decidedly striking and picturesque. Much of the marketing is also brought down from the mountains on donkeys, mules, small horses and horned cattle. In the management of these animals we see in Haiti a cruelty inherited from the old slave system. They often beat them unmercifully.

I have said that the men did not strike me as equal to the women, and I think that this is largely due to the fact that most of the men are compelled to spend much of their lives as soldiers in the service of their country, and this is a life often fatal to the growth of all manly qualities. Every third man you meet within the streets of Port au Prince is a soldier. His vocation is unnatural. He is separated from home and industry. He is tempted to spend much of his time in gambling, drinking and other destructive vices; vices which never fail to show themselves repulsively in the manners and forms of those addicted to them. As I walked through the streets of Port au Prince and saw these marred, shattered and unmanly men, I found myself taking up over Haiti the lament of Jesus over Jerusalem, and saying to myself, "Haiti! Poor Haiti! When will she learn and practice the things that make for her peace and happiness?"

No other land has brighter skies. No other land has purer water, richer soil, or a more happily diversified climate. She has all the natural conditions essential to a noble, prosperous and happy country. Yet, there she is, torn and rent by revolutions, by clamorous factions and anarchies; floundering her life away from year in a labyrinth of social misery. Every little while we find her convulsed by civil war, engaged in the terrible work of death; frantically shedding her own blood and driving her best mental material into hopeless exile. Port au Prince, a city of sixty thousand souls, and capable of being made one of the healthiest, happiest and one of the most beautiful cities of the West Indies, has been destroyed by fire once in each twenty-five years of its history. The explanation is this: Haiti is a country of revolutions. They break forth without warning and without excuse. The town may stand at sunset and vanish in the morning. Splendid ruins, once the homes of the rich, meet us on every street. Great warehouses, once the property of successful merchants, confront us with their marred and shattered walls in different parts of the city. When we ask: "Whence these mournful ruins?" and "Why are they not rebuilt?" we are answered by one word—a word of agony and dismal terror, a word which goes to the core of all this people's woes; It is, "revolution!" Such are the uncertainties and insecurities caused by this revolutionary madness of a part of her people, that no insurance company will insure property at a rate which the holder can afford to pay. Under such a condition of things a tranquil mind is impossible. There is ever a chronic, feverish looking forward to possible disasters. Incendiary fires; fires set on foot as a proof of dissatisfaction with the government; fires for personal revenge, and fires to promote revolution are of startling frequency. This is sometimes thought to be due to the character of the race. Far from it. The common people of Haiti are peaceful enough. They have no taste for revolutions. The fault is not with the ignorant many, but with the educated and ambitious few. Too proud to work, and not disposed to go into commerce, they make politics a business of their country. Governed neither by love nor mercy for their country, they care not into what depths she may be plunged. No president, however virtuous, wise and patriotic, ever suits them when they themselves happen to be out of power.

I wish I could say that these are the only conspirators against the peace of Haiti, but I cannot. They have allies in the United States. Recent developments have shown that even a former United States Minister, resident and Consul General to that country has considered against the present government of Haiti. It so happens that we have men in this country who, to accomplish their personal and selfish ends, will fan the flame of passion between the factions in Haiti and will otherwise assist in setting revolutions afoot. To their shame be it spoken, men in high American quarters have boasted to me of their ability to start a revolution in Haiti at pleasure. They have only to raise sufficient money, they say, with which to arm and otherwise equip the malcontents, of either faction, to effect their object. Men who have old munitions of war or old ships to sell; ships that will go down in the first storm, have an interest in stirring up strife in Haiti. It gives them a market for their worthless wares. Others of a speculative turn of mind and who have money to lend at high rates of interest are glad to conspire with revolutionary chiefs of either faction, to enable them to start a bloody insurrection. To them, the welfare of Haiti is nothing; the shedding of human blood is nothing; the success of free institutions is nothing, and the ruin of neighboring country is nothing. They are sharks, pirates and Shylocks, greedy for money, no matter at what cost of life and misery to mankind.

It is the opinion of many, and it is mine as well, that these revolutions would be less frequent if there were less impunity afforded the leaders of them. The so-called right of asylum is extended to them. This right is merciful to the few, but cruel to the many. While these crafty plotters of mischief fail in their revolutionary attempts, they can escape the consequences of their treason and rebellion by running into the foreign legations and consulates. Once within the walls of these, the right of asylum prevails and they know that they are safe from pursuit and will be permitted to leave the country without bodily harm. If I were a citizen of Haiti, I would do all I could to abolish this right of Asylum. During the late trouble at Port au Prince, I had under the protection of the American flag twenty of the insurgents who, after doing their mischief, were all safely embarked to Kingston without punishment, and since then have again plotted against the peace of their country. The strange thing is, that neither the government nor the rebels are in favor of the abolition of this so-called right of asylum, because the fortunes of war may at some time make it convenient to the one or the other of them to find such shelter.

Manifestly, this revolutionary spirit of Haiti is her curse, her crime, her greatest calamity and the explanation of the limited condition of her civilization. It makes her an object of distress to her friends at home and abroad. It reflects upon the colored race everywhere. Many who would have gladly believed in her ability to govern herself wisely and successfully are compelled at times to bow their heads in doubt and despair. Certain it is that while this evil spirit shall prevail, Haiti cannot rise very high in the scale of civilization. While this shall prevail, ignorance and superstition will flourish and no good thing can grow and prosper within her borders. While this shall prevail, she will resemble the man cutting himself among the tombs. While this shall prevail, her rich and fruitful soil will bring forth briers, thorns and noxious weeds. While this evil spirit shall prevail, her great natural wealth will be wasted and her splendid possibilities will be blasted. While this spirit shall prevail, she will sadden the hearts of her friends and rejoice the hearts of her enemies. While this spirit of turbulence shall prevail, confidence in her public men will be weakened, and her well-won independence will be threatened. Schemes of aggression and foreign protectorates will be invented. While this evil spirit shall prevail, faith in the value and stability of her institutions, so essential to the happiness and well-being of her people, will vanish. While it shall prevail, the arm of her industry will be paralyzed, the spirit of enterprise will languish, national opportunities will be neglected, the means of education will be limited, the ardor of patriotism will be quenched, her national glory will be tarnished, and her hopes and the hopes of her friends will be blighted.

In its presence, commerce is interrupted, progress halts, streams go unbridged, highways go unrepaired, streets go unpaved, cities go unlighted, filth accumulates in her marketplaces, evil smells affront the air, and disease and pestilence are invited to their work of sorrow, pain and death.

Port au Prince should be one of the finest cities in the world. There is no natural cause for its present condition. No city in the world is by nature more easily drained of impurities and kept clean. The land slopes to the water's edge, and pure sparkling mountain streams flow through its streets on their way to the sea. With peace firmly established within her borders, this city might be as healthy as New York, and Haiti might easily lead all the other islands of the Caribbean Sea in the race of civilization.

You will ask me about the President of Haiti. I will tell you. Whatever may be said or thought of him to the contrary I affirm that there is no man in Haiti, who more fully understands or more deeply feels the need of peace in his country than does President Hyppolite. No purer patriot ever ruled the country. His administration, from the first to the last, has had the welfare of his country in view. It is against the fierce revolutionary spirit of a part of his countrymen that he has had to constantly watch and contend. It has met him more fiercely at the seat of his government than elsewhere.

Unhappily, his countrymen are not his only detractors. Though a friend and benefactor of his country, and though bravely battling against conspiracy, treason and rebellion, instead of receiving the sympathy and support of the American Press and people, this man has been denounced as a cruel monster. I declare to you, than this, no judgment of President Hyppolite could be more unjust and more undeserved.

I know him well and have studied his character with care, and no man can look into his thoughtful face and hear his friendly voice without feeling that he is in the presence of a kind hearted man. The picture of him in the New York papers, which some of you have doubtless seen, does him no manner of justice, and, in fact, does him startling injustice. It makes him appear like a brute, while he is in truth a fine looking man, "black, but comely." His features are regular, his bearing dignified, his manner polished, and he makes for himself the impression of a gentleman and a scholar. His conduct during the recent troubles in Haiti was indeed, prompt, stern and severe, but, in the judgment of the most thoughtful and patriotic citizens of that country, it was not more stringent than the nature of the case required. Here, as elsewhere, desperate cases require desperate remedies. Governments must be a terror to evildoers if they would be praised to those who do well. It will no do for a government with the knife of treason at its throat, to bear the sword in vain.

I invoke for the President of Haiti the charity and justice we once demanded for our President. Like Abraham Lincoln, President

Hyppolite was duly elected President of Haiti and took the oath of office prescribed by his country, and when treason and rebellion raised their destructive heads, he like Mr. Lincoln, struck them down otherwise he would have been struck down by them.

Hyppolite did the same. If one should be commended for his patriotism, so should the other. While representing the United States in Haiti, I was repeatedly charged in certain quarters, with being a friend to Haiti. I am not ashamed of that charge. I own at once, that the charge is true, and I would be ashamed to have it otherwise than true. I am indeed a friend to Haiti, but not in the sense my accusers would have you believe. They would have it that I preferred the interest of Haiti, to the just claims of my own country, and this charge I utterly deny and defy any man to prove it. I am a friend of Haiti and a friend of every other people upon whom the yoke of slavery had been imposed. In this I only stand with philanthropic men and women everywhere. I am the friend of Haiti in the same sense in which General Harrison, the President of the United States, himself is a friend of Haiti. I am glad to be able to say here and now of him, that I found in President Harrison no trace of the vulgar prejudice which is just now so malignant in some parts of our southern country towards the Negro. He sent me not to represent in Haiti our race prejudice, but the best sentiments of our loyal, liberty-loving American people. No mean or mercenary mission was set before me. His advice to me was worthy of his lofty character. He authorized me in substance to do all that I could consistently with my duty to the United States, for the welfare of Haiti and, as far as I could, to persuade her to value and preserve her free institutions, and to remove all ground for there proaches now hurled at her and at the colored race through her example.

The language of the President was worthy of the chief magistrate of the American people—a people who should be too generous to profit by the misfortune of others; too proud to stoop to meanness; to honest to practice duplicity; too strong to menace the weak, and every way too great to be small. I went to Haiti, imbued with the noble sentiments of General Harrison. For this reason, with others, I named him as worthy to be his own successor, and I could have named no other more worthy of the honor.

From the beginning of our century until now, Haiti and its inhabitants under one aspect or another, have, for various reasons, been very much in the thoughts of the American people. While slavery existed amongst us, her example was a sharp thorn in our side and a source of alarm and terror. She came into the sisterhood of nations through blood. She was described at the time of her advent, as a very hell of horrors. Her very name was pronounced with a shudder. She was a

startling and frightful surprise and a threat to all slaveholders throughout the world, and the slaveholding world has had its questioning eye
upon her career ever since.

By reason of recent events and abolition of slavery, the enfranchisement of the Negro in our country, and the probable completion of
the Nicaragua canal, Haiti has under another aspect, become, of late,
interesting to American statesmen. More thought, more ink and paper
have been devoted to her than to all the other West India Islands put
together. This interest is both political and commercial, for Haiti is
increasingly important in both respects. But aside from politics and
aside from commerce, there is, perhaps, no equal number of people
anywhere on the globe, in whose history, character and destiny there
is more to awaken sentiment, thought and inquiry, than is found in the
history of her people.

The country itself, apart from its people, has special attractions. First
things have ever had a peculiar and romantic interest, simply because
they are first things. In this, Haiti is fortunate. She has in many things
been first. She has been made the theatre of great events. She was the
first of all the cis-Atlantic world, upon which the firm foot of the progressive, aggressive and all-conquering white man was permanently set.
Her grand old tropical forests, fields and mountains, were among the
first of the New World to have their silence broken by trans-Atlantic
song and speech. She was the first to be invaded by the Christian
religion and to witness its forms and ordinances. She was the first to
see a Christian church and to behold the cross of Christ. She was also
the first to witness the bitter agonies of the Negro bending under the
blood-stained lash of Christian slaveholders. Happily too, for her, she
was the first of the New World in which the black man asserted his
right to be free and was brave enough to fight for his freedom and
fortunate enough to gain it.

In thinking of Haiti, a painful, perplexing and contradictory fact
meets us at the outset. It is: that Negro slavery was brought to the New
World by the same people from whom Haiti received her religion and
her civilization. No people have ever shown greater religious zeal or
have given more attention to the ordinances of the Christian church
than have the Spaniards; yet no people were ever guilty of more injustice and blood-chilling cruelty to their fellowmen than these same
religious Spaniards. Men more learned in the theory of religion than I
am, may be able to explain and reconcile these two facts; but to me they
seem to prove that men may be very pious, and yet very pitiless; very
religious and yet practice the foulest crimes. These Spanish Christians
found in Haiti a million of harmless men and women, and in less than
sixty years they had murdered nearly all of them. With religion on their

lips, the tiger in their hearts and the slave whip in their hands, they
lashed these innocent natives to toil, death and extinction. When these
pious souls had destroyed the natives, they opened the släve-trade with
Africa as a merciful device. Such, at least, is the testimony of history.

Interesting as Haiti is in being the cradle in which American religion and civilization were first rocked, its present inhabitants are still
more interesting as having been actors in great moral and social events.
These have been scarcely less portentous and startling than the terrible earthquakes which have sometimes moved their mountains and
shaken down their towns and cities. The conditions in which the Republican Government of Haiti originated, were peculiar. The great
fact concerning its people, is, that they were Negro slaves and by force
conquered their masters and made themselves free and independent.
As a people thus made free and having remained so for eighty-seven
years, they are now asked to justify their assumption of statehood at
the bar of the civilized world by conduct becoming a civilized nation.

The ethnologist observes them with curious eyes, and questions
them on the ground of race. The statesman questions their ability to
govern themselves; while the scholar and philanthropist are interested
in their progress, their improvement and the question of their destiny.

But, interesting as they are to all these and to others, the people of
Haiti, by reason of ancestral identity, are more interesting to the colored
people of the United States than to all others, for the Negro, like the
Jew, can never part with his identity and race. Color does for the one
what religion does for the other and makes both distinct from the rest
of mankind. No matter where prosperity or misfortune may chance to
drive the Negro, he is identified with and shares the fortune of his race.
We are told to go to Haiti; to go to Africa. Neither Haiti nor Africa can
save us from common doom. Whether we are here or there, we must
rise or fall with the race. Hence, we can do about as much for Africa or
Haiti by good conduct and success here as anywhere else in the world.
The talk of the bettering ourselves by getting rid of the white race, is
a great mistake. It is about as idle for the black man to think of getting
rid of the white man, as it is for the white man to think of getting rid of
the black. They are just the two races which cannot be excluded from
any part of the globe, nor can they exclude each other; so we might as
well decide to live together here as to go elsewhere. Besides, for obvious
reasons, until we can make ourselves respected in the United States, we
shall not be respected in Haiti, Africa, or anywhere else.

Of my regard and friendship for Haiti, I have already spoken. I have,
too, already spoken somewhat of her faults, as well, for they are many
and grievous. I shall, however, show before I get through, that, with all
her faults, you and I and all of us have reason to respect Haiti for her

services to the cause of liberty and human equality throughout the world, and for the noble qualities she exhibited in all the trying conditions of her early history.

I have, since my return to the United States, been pressed on all sides to foretell what will be the future of Haiti-whether she will ever master and subdue the turbulent elements within her borders and become an orderly Republic. Whether she will maintain her liberty and independence, or, at last, part with both and become a subject of some one or another of the powerful nations of the world by which she seems to be coveted. The question still further is, whether she will fall away into anarchy, chaos and barbarism, or rise to the dignity and happiness of a highly civilized nation and be a credit to the colored race? I am free to say that I believe she will fulfill the latter condition and destiny. By one class of writers, however, such as Mr. Froude and his echoes, men and women who write what they know the prejudice of the hour will accept and pay for, this question has been vehemently answered already against Haiti and the possibilities of the Negro race generally.

They tell us that Haiti is already doomed—that she is on the downgrade to barbarism; and, worse still, they affirm that when the Negro is left to himself there or elsewhere, he inevitably gravitates to barbarism. Alas, for poor Haiti! and alas, for the poor Negro everywhere, if this shall prove true!

The argument as stated against Haiti, is, that since her freedom, she has become lazy; that she is given to gross idolatry, and that these evils are on the increase. That voodooism, fetishism, serpent worship and cannibalism are prevalent there; that little children are fatted for slaughter and offered as sacrifices to their voodoo deities; that large boys and girls run naked through the streets of the towns and cities, and that things are generally going from bad to worse.

In reply to these dark and damning allegations, it will be sufficient only to make a general statement. I admit at once, that there is much ignorance and much superstition in Haiti. The common people there believe much in divinations, charms, witchcraft, putting spells on each other, and in the supernatural and miracle working power of their voodoo priests generally. Owing to this, there is a feeling of superstition and dread of each other, the destructive tendency of which cannot be exaggerated. But it is amazing how much of such darkness society has borne and can bear and is bearing without falling to pieces and without being hopelessly abandoned to barbarism.

Let it be remembered that superstition and idolatry in one form or another have not been in the past, nor are they in the present, confined to any particular place or locality, and that, even in our enlightened age, we need not travel far from our own country, from England, from

Scotland, from Ireland, France, Germany or Spain to find considerable traces of gross superstition. We consult familiar spirits in America.
Queen Victoria gets water from the Jordan to christen her children, as
if the water of that river were any better than the water of any other
river. Many go thousands of miles in this age of light to see an old seam-
less coat supposed to have some divine virtue. Christians at Rome kiss
the great toe of a black image called St. Peter, and go up stairs on their
knees, to gain divine favor. Here, we build houses and call them God's
houses, and go into them to meet God, as if the Almighty dwelt in
temples made with men's hands. I am not, myself, altogether free from
superstition. I would rather sit at a table with twelve persons than at one
with thirteen; and would rather see the new moon first over my right
shoulder than over my left, though my reason tells me that it makes no
manner of difference over which shoulder I see the new moon or the
old. And what better is the material of one house than that of another?

Can man build a house more holy than the house which God himself has built for the children of men? If men are denied a future
civilization because of superstition, there are others than the people
of Haiti who must be so denied. In one form or another, superstition
will be found everywhere and among all sorts of people, high or low.
New England once believed in witches, and yet she has become highly
civilized.

Haiti is charged with the terrible crime of sacrificing little children
to her voodoo gods, and you will want to know what I have to say
about this shocking allegation. My answer is: That while I lived in Haiti
I made diligent inquiry about this alleged practice so full of horror. I
questioned many persons concerning it, but I never met a man who
could say that he ever saw an instance of the kind; nor did I ever see a
man who ever met any other man who said he had seen such an act of
human sacrifice. This I know is not conclusive, for strange things have
sometimes been done in the name of God, and in the practice of religion. You know that our good father Abraham (not Abraham Lincoln)
once thought that it would please Jehovah to have him kill his son Isaac
and offer him a sacrifice on the altar. Men in all ages have thought to
gain divine favor of their divinities or to escape their wrath by offering
up to them something of great and special value. Sometimes it was the
firstlings of the flock, and sometimes it was the fat of fed beasts, fed for
the purpose of having it nice and acceptable to the divine being. As if
a divine being could be greatly pleased with the taste or smell of such
offerings. Men have become more sensible of late. They keep, smell and
eat their fat beef and mutton themselves.

As to the little boys and girls running nude in the streets, I have to
say, that while there are instances of the kind, and more of them we,

with the ideas of our latitude, would easily tolerate, they are never-theless the exceptions to the general rule in Haiti. You will see in the streets of Port au Prince, one hundred decently dressed children to one that is nude; yet, our newspaper correspondents and six-day tour-ists in Haiti, would lead you to think that nudity is there the rule and decent clothing the exception. It should be remembered also, that in a warm climate like that of Haiti, the people consider more the comfort of their children in this respect than any fear of improper exposure of their little innocent bodies.

A word about snake worship. This practice is not new in the history of religion. It is as old as Egypt and is a part of our own religious system. Moses lifted up the serpent in the wilderness as a remedy for a great malady, and our Bible tells us of some wonderful things done by the ser-pent in the way of miraculous healing. Besides, he seems to have been on hand and performed marvelous feats in the Garden of Eden, and to have wielded a potent and mysterious influence in deciding the fate of mankind for time and eternity. Without the snake, the plan of salvation itself would not be complete. No wonder then that Haiti, having heard so much of the serpent in these respectable quarters and sublime rela-tions, has acquired some respect for a divinity so potent and so ancient.

But the future of Haiti. What is it to be? Will it be civilization or barbarism? Will she remain an independent state, or be swallowed up by one or another of the great states? Whither is she tending? In con-sidering these questions, we should allow no prejudice to influence us on the one hand or the other. If it be true that the Negro, left to him-self, lapses into barbarism, as is alleged; the Negro above and beyond all others in the world should know it and should acknowledge it.

But it is said that the people of Haiti are lazy. Well, with the condi-tions of existence so easy and the performance of work so uninviting, the wonder is not that the men of Haiti are lazy, but that they work at all. But it is not true that the people of Haiti are as lazy as they are usually represented to be. There is much hard work done in Haiti, both mental and physical. This is true, not only of accessible altitudes where the air is cool and bracing, but it is so in the low lands, where the climate is hot, parching and enervating. No one can see the ships afloat in the splendid harbors of Haiti, and see the large imports and exports of the country, without seeing also that somebody there has been at work. A revenue of millions does not come to a country where no work is done.

Plainly enough; we should take no snap judgment on a question so momentous. It should not be determined by a dash of the pen and upon mere appearances of the moment. There are ebbs and flows in the tide of human affairs, and Haiti is no exception to this rule. There have been times in her history when she gave promise of great progress, and others, when she seemed to retrograde. We should view her in the light broad light of her whole history, and observe well her conduct in the various vicissitudes through which she has passed. Upon such broad view I am sure Haiti will be vindicated.

It was once said by the great Daniel O'Connell, that the history of Ireland might be traced, like a wounded man through a crowd, by the blood. The same may be said of the history of Haiti as a free state. Her liberty was born in blood, cradled in misfortune, and has lived more or less in a storm of revolutionary turbulence. It is important to know how she behaved in these storms. As I view it, there is one great fundamental and soul-cheering fact concerning her. It is this: Despite all the trying vicissitudes of her history, despite all the machinations of her enemies at home, in spite of all temptations from abroad, despite all her many destructive revolutions, she has remained true to herself, true to her autonomy, and still remains a free and independent state. No power on this broad earth has yet induced or seduced her to seek a foreign protector, or has compelled her to bow her proud neck to a foreign government. We talk of assuming protectorate over Haiti. We had better not attempt it. The success of such an enterprise is repelled by her whole history. She would rather abandon her ports and harbors, retire to her mountain fastnesses, or burn her towns and shed her warm, red, tropical blood over their ashes than to submit to the degradation of any foreign yoke, however friendly. In whatever may be the sources of her shame and misfortune, she has one source of great complacency; she lives proudly in the glory of her bravely won liberty and her blood bought independence, and no hostile foreign foot has been allowed to tread her scared soil in peace from the hour of her independence until now. Her future autonomy is at least secure. Whether civilized or savage, whatever the future may have in store for her, Haiti is the black man's country, now forever.

In just vindication of Haiti, I can go one step further. I can speak of her, not only words of admiration, but words of gratitude as well. She has grandly served the cause of universal human liberty. We should not forget that the freedom you and I enjoy today; that the freedom that eight hundred thousand colored people enjoy in the British West Indies; the freedom that has come to the colored race the world over, is largely due to the brave stand taken by the black sons of Haiti ninety years ago. When they struck for freedom, they builded better than they knew. Their swords were not drawn and could not be drawn simply for themselves alone. They were linked and interlinked with their race, and striking for their freedom, they struck for the freedom of every black man in the world.

It is said of ancient nations, that each had its special mission in the world and that each taught the world some important lesson. The Jews taught the world a religion, a sublime conception of the Deity. The Greeks taught the world philosophy and beauty. The Romans taught the world jurisprudence. England is foremost among the modern nations in commerce and manufactures. Germany has taught the world to think, while the American Republic is giving the world an example of a Government by the people, of the people and for the people. Among these large bodies, the little community of Haiti, anchored in the Caribbean Sea, has had her mission in the world, and a mission which the world had much need to learn. She has taught the world the danger of slavery and the value of liberty. In this respect she has been the greatest of all our modern teachers.

Speaking for the Negro, I can say, we owe much to Walker for his appeal; to John Brown for the blow struck at Harper's Ferry, to Lundy and Garrison for their advocacy. We owe much especially to Thomas Clarkson, to William Wilberforce, to Thomas Fowell Buxton, and to the anti-slavery societies at home and abroad; but we owe incomparably more to Haiti than to them all. I regard her as the original pioneer emancipator of the nineteenth century. It was her one brave example that first of all started the Christian world into a sense of the Negro's manhood. It was she who first awoke the Christian world to a sense of "the danger of goading too far the energy that slumbers in a black man's arm." Until Haiti struck for freedom, the conscience of the Christian world slept profoundly over slavery. It was scarcely troubled even by a dream of this crime against justice and liberty. The Negro was in its estimation a sheep like creature, having no rights which white men were bound to respect, a docile animal, a kind of ass, capable of bearing burdens, and receiving strips from a white master without resentment, and without resistance. The mission of Haiti was to dispel this degradation and dangerous delusion, and to give to the world a new and true revelation of the black man's character. This mission she has performed and performed it well.

Until she spoke no Christian nation had abolished Negro slavery. Until she spoke no Christian nation had given to the world an organized effort to abolish slavery. Until she spoke the slave ship, followed by hungry sharks, greedy to devour the dead and dying slaves flung overboard to feed them, ploughed in peace the South Atlantic painting the sea with the Negro's blood. Until she spoke, the slave-trade was sanctioned by all the Christian nations of the world, and our land of liberty and light included. Men made fortunes by this infernal traffic, and were esteemed as good Christians, and the standing types and representations of the Savior of the World. Until Haiti spoke, the church was silent, and the pulpit was dumb. Slave-traders lived and slave-traders died. Funeral sermons were preached over them, and of them it was said that they died in the triumphs of the Christian faith and went to heaven among the just.

To have any just conception or measurement of the intelligence, solidarity and manly courage of the people of Haiti when under the lead of Toussaint L'Ouverture, and the dauntless Dessalines, you must remember what the conditions were by which they were surrounded; that all the neighboring islands were slaveholding, and that to no one of all these islands could she look for sympathy, support and cooperation. She trod the wine press alone. Her hand was against the Christian world, and the hand of the Christian world was against her. Hers was a forlorn hope, and she knew that she must do or die.

In Greek or Roman history nobler daring cannot be found. It will ever be a matter of wonder and astonishment to thoughtful men, that a people in abject slavery, subject to the lash, and kept in ignorance of letters, as these slaves were, should have known enough, or have had left in them enough manhood, to combine, to organize, and to select for themselves trusted leaders and with loyal hearts to follow them into the jaws of death to obtain liberty.

In forecasting the future of this people, then, I insist that some importance shall be given to this and to another grand initial fact: that the freedom of Haiti was not given as a boon, but conquered as a right! Her people fought for it. They suffered for it, and thousands of them endured the most horrible tortures, and perished for it. It is well said that a people to whom freedom is given can never wear it as grandly as can they who have fought and suffered to gain it. Here, as elsewhere, what comes easily, is liable to go easily. But what man will fight to gain, that, man will fight to maintain. To this test Haiti was early subjected, and she stood this test like pure gold.

To re-enslave her brave self-emancipated sons of liberty, France sent in round number's, to Haiti during the years 1802–1803, 50,000 of her veteran troops, commanded by the most experienced and skillful generals. History tells us what became of these brave and skillful warriors from France. It shows that they shared the fate of Pharaoh and his hosts. Negro manhood, Negro bravery, Negro military genius and skill, assisted by yellow fever and pestilence made short work of them. The souls of them by thousands were speedily sent into eternity, and their bones were scattered on the mountains of Haiti, there to bleach, burn and vanish under the fierce tropical sun. Since 1804 Haiti has maintained national independence. I fling these facts at the feet of the detractors of the Negro and of Haiti. They may help them to solve the problem of her future. They not only indicate the Negro's courage, but demonstrate his intelligence as well.

No better test of the intelligence of people can be had than is furnished in their laws, their institutions and their great men. To produce these in any considerable degree of perfection, a high order of ability is always required. Haiti has no cause to shrink from this test or from any other.

Human greatness is classified in three divisions: first, greatness of administration; second greatness of organization; and the third, greatness of discovery, the latter being the highest order of human greatness. In all three of these divisions, Haiti appears to advantage. Her Toussaint L'Ouvertures, her Dessalines, her Christophes, her Petions, her Reguad and others, their enemies being judges, were men of decided ability. They were great in all the three departments of human greatness. Let any man in our highly favored country, undertake to organize an army of raw recruits, and especially let any colored man undertake to organize men of his own color, and subject them to military discipline, and he will at once see the hard task that Haiti had on hand, in resisting France and slavery, and be held to admire the ability and character displayed by the sons in making and managing her armies and achieving her freedom.

But Haiti did more than raise armies and discipline troops. She organized a Government and maintained a Government during eighty-seven years. Though she has been ever and anon swept by whirlwinds of lawless turbulence; though she has been shaken by earthquakes of anarchy at home, and has encountered the chilling blasts of prejudice and hate from the outside world, though she has been assailed by fire and sword, from without and within, she has, through all the machinations of her enemies, maintained a well defined civil government, and maintains it today. She is represented at all courts of Europe, by able men, and, in turn, she has representatives from all the nations of Europe in her capitol.

She has her judiciary, her executive and legislative departments. She has her house of representatives and her senate. All the functions of government have been, and are now being, regularly performed within her domain. What does all this signify? I answer. Very much to her credit. If it be true that all present, and all the future rests upon all the past, there is a solid ground to hope for Haiti. There is a fair chance that she may yet be highly progressive, prosperous and happy.

Those who have studied the history of civilization, with the largest range of observation and the most profound philosophical generalization, tell us that men are governed by their antecedents; that what they did under one condition of affairs they will be likely to do under similar conditions, whenever such shall arise. Haiti has in the past, raised many learned, able and patriotic men. She has made wise laws for her

own government. Among her citizens she has had scholars and statesmen, learned editors, able lawyers and eminent physicians. She has now,
men of education in the church and in her government, and she is now,
as ever, in the trend of civilization. She may be slow and halting in the
race, but her face is in the right direction.

The statement that she is on the down grade to barbarism is easily
made, but hard to sustain. It is not all borne out by my observation and
experience while in that country. It is my good fortune to possess the
means of comparison, as to "what Haiti was and what Haiti is;" what
she was twenty years ago, and what she is now. I visited that country
twenty years ago and have spent much time there since, and I have no
hesitation in saying that, with all that I have said of her revolutions and
defective civilization, I can report a marked and gratifying improvement in the condition of her people, now, compared with what it was
twenty years ago.

In port au prince, which may be taken as a fair expression of the general condition of the country, I saw more apparent domestic happiness,
more wealth, more personal neatness, more attention to dress, more
carriage rolling through the streets, more commercial activity, more
schools, more well clothed and well cared for children, more churches,
more teachers, more Sisters of Charity more respect for marriage, more
family comfort, more attention to sanitary conditions, more and better water supply, more and better Catholic clergy, more attention to
religious observances, more elegant residences, and more of everything
desirable than I saw there twenty years ago.

At that time Haiti was isolated. She was outside of telegraphic communication with the civilized world. She now has such connection. She
has paid for a cable of her own and with her own money.

This has been accomplished under the much-abused President Hyppolite. Then, there was no effort to light any of the streets. Now, the
main streets are lighted. The streets are full of carriages at night, but
none are allowed to appear without lighted lamps, and every attention
is given to the peace and good order of the citizens. There is much
loud talk in Haiti, but blows are seldom exchanged between Haitians.

Even her revolutions are less sanguinary and ruthless now, than formerly. They have in many cases been attended with great disregard
of private rights, with destruction of property and the commission of
other crimes, but nothing of the kind was permitted to occur in the
revolution by which President Hyppolite, was raised to power. He was
inaugurated in a manner as orderly as that inducting into office any
President of the United States.

Before we decide against the probability of progress in Haiti, we
should look into the history of the progress of other nations. Some of

the most enlightened and highly civilized states of the world of today, were, a few centuries ago, as deeply depraved in morals, manners and customs, as Haiti is alleged to be now. Prussia, which is today the arbiter of peace and war in Europe and holds in her borders the profoundest thinkers of the nineteenth century, was, only three centuries ago, like Haiti, the theatre of warring factions, and the scene of flagrant immoralities. France, England, Italy and Spain have all gone through the strife and turmoil of factional war, the like of which now makes Haiti a by-word, and a hissing to a mocking earth. As they have passed through the period of violence, why may not Haiti do the same?

It should also be remembered that Haiti is still in her childhood. Given her time! Give her time!! While eighty years may be a good old age for a man, it can only be as a year in the life of a nation. With a people beginning a national life as Haiti did, with such crude material within, and such antagonistic forces operating upon her from without, the marvel is, not that she is far in the rear of civilization, but that she has survived in any sense as a civilized nation.

Though she is still an infant, she is out of the arms of her mother. Though she creeps, rather than walks; stumbles often and sometimes falls, her head is not broken, and she still lives and grows, and I predict, will yet be tall and strong. Her wealth is greater, her population is larger, her credit is higher, her currency is sounder, her progress is surer, her statesmen are abler, her patriotism is nobler, and her government is steadier and firmer than twenty years ago. I predict that out of civil strife, revolution and war, there will come a desire for peace. Out of division will come a desire for union; out of weakness a desire for strength, out of ignorance a desire for knowledge, and out of stagnation will come a desire for progress. Already I find in her a longing for peace. Already she feels that she has had enough and more than enough of war. Already she perceives the need of education, and is providing means to obtain it on a large scale. Already she has added five hundred schools to her forces of education, within the two years of Hyppolite's administration. In the face of such facts; in the face of the fact that Haiti still lives, after being boycotted by all the Christian world; in the face of the fact of her known progress within the last twenty years in the face of the fact that she has attached herself to the car of the world's civilization, I will not, I cannot believe that her star is to go out in darkness, but I will rather believe that whatever may happen of peace or war Haiti will remain in the firmament of nations, and, like the star of the north, will shine on and shine on forever.

Self-Made Men
(1894)

In this motivational masterpiece, Frederick Douglass provides and inspirational account of his own rise from slavery to success, while providing an explanation of how the key to overcoming even the lowest of origins is, in his words, "Work! Work!! Work!!! Work!!!!" While Douglass spoke on this subject many times throughout his life, the following address was delivered on April 6, 1894, just 10 months before his death, at the Indian Industrial School in Carlisle, Pennsylvania.

The subject announced for this evening's entertainment is not new. Man in one form or another, has been a frequent and fruitful subject for the press, the pulpit and the platform. This subject has come up for consideration under a variety of attractive titles, such as "Great Men," "Representative Men," "Peculiar Men," "Scientific Men," "Literary Men," "Successful Men," "Men of Genius," and "Men of the World;" but under whatever name or designation, the vital point of interest in the discussion has ever been the same, and that is, manhood itself, and this in its broadest and most comprehensive sense.

This tendency to the universal, in such discussion, is altogether natural and all controlling; for when we consider what man, as a whole, is; what he has been; what he aspires to be, and what, by a wise and vigorous cultivation of his faculties, he may yet become, we see that it leads irresistibly to this broad view of him as a subject of thought and inquiry.

The saying of the poet that "The proper study of mankind is man," and which has been the starting point of so many lectures, essays and speeches, holds its place, like all other great utterances, because it contains a great truth and a truth alike for every age and generation of men. It is always new and can never grow old. It is neither dimmed by time nor tarnished by repetition; for man, both in respect of himself and of his species, is now, and evermore will be, the center of unsatisfied human curiosity.

The pleasure we derive from any department of knowledge is largely due to the glimpse which it gives to us of our own nature. We may travel far over land and sea, brave all climates, dare all dangers, endure all hardships, try all latitudes and longitudes; we may penetrate the earth, sound the ocean's depths and sweep the hollow sky with our glasses, in the pursuit of other knowledge; we may contemplate the glorious landscape gemmed by forest, lake and river and dotted with peaceful homes and quiet herds; we may whirl away to the great cities, all aglow with life and enterprise; we may mingle with the imposing assemblages of wealth and power; we may visit the halls where Art works her miracles in music, speech and color, and where Science unbars the gates to higher planes of civilization; but no matter how radiant the colors, how enchanting the melody, how gorgeous and splendid the pageant; man himself, with eyes turned inward upon his own wondrous attributes and powers surpasses them all. A single human soul standing here upon the margin we call TIME, overlooking, in the vastness of its range, the solemn past which can neither be recalled nor remodelled, ever chafing against finite limitations, entangled with interminable contradictions, eagerly seeking to scan the invisible past and to pierce the clouds and darkness of the ever mysterious future, has attractions for thought and study, more numerous and powerful than all other objects beneath the sky. To human thought and inquiry he is broader than all visible worlds, loftier than all heights and deeper than all depths. Were I called upon to point out the broadest and most permanent distinction between mankind and other animals, it would be this; their earnest desire for the fullest knowledge of human nature on all its many sides. The importance of this knowledge is immeasurable, and by no other is human life so affected and colored. Nothing can bring to man so much of happiness or so much of misery as man himself. Today he exalts himself to heaven by his virtues and achievements; tomorrow he smiles with sadness and pain, by his crimes and follies. But whether exalted or debased, charitable or wicked; whether saint or villain, priest or prize fighter; if only he be great in his line, he is an unfailing source of interest, as one of a common brotherhood; for the best man finds in his breast the evidence of kinship with the worst, and the worst with the best. Confront us with either extreme and you will rivet our attention and fix us in earnest contemplation, for our chief desire is to know what there is in man and to know him at all extremes and ends and opposites, and for this knowledge, or for the want of it, we will follow him from the gates of life to the gates of death, and beyond them.

As this subject can never become old, so it can never be exhausted. Man is too closely related to the Infinite to be divided, weighed, measured and reduced to fixed standards, and thus adjusted to finite comprehension. No two of anything are exactly alike, and what is true of man in one generation may lack some degree of truth in another, but his distinctive qualities as man, are inherent and remain forever. Progressive in his nature, he defies the power of progress to overtake him to make known, definitely, the limits of his marvellous powers and possibilities.

From man comes all that we know or can imagine of heaven and earth, of time and eternity. He is the prolific constituter of manners, morals, religions and governments. He spins them out as the spider spins his web, and they are coarse or fine, kind or cruel, according to the degree of intelligence reached by him at the period of their establishment. He compels us to contemplate his past with wonder and to survey his future with much the same feelings as those with which Columbus is supposed to have gazed westward over the sea. It is the faith of the race that in man there exists far outlying continents of power, thought and feeling, which remain to be discovered, explored, cultivated, made practical and glorified.

Mr. Emerson has declared that it is natural to believe in great men. Whether this is a fact, or not, we do believe in them and worship them. The Visible God of the New Testament is revealed to us as a man of like passions with ourselves. We seek out our wisest and best man, the man who, by eloquence or the sword compels us to believe him such, and make him our leader, prophet, preacher and law giver. We do this, not because he is essentially different from us, but because of his identity with us. He is our best representative and reflects, on a colossal scale, the scale to which we would aspire, our highest aims, objects, powers and possibilities.

This natural reverence for all that is great in man, and this tendency to deify and worship him, though natural and the source of man's elevation, has not always shown itself wise but has often shown itself far otherwise than wise. It has often given us a wicked ruler for a righteous one, a false prophet for a true one, a corrupt preacher for a pure one, a man of war for a man of peace, and a distorted and vengeful image of God for an image of justice and mercy.

But it is not my purpose to attempt here any comprehensive and exhaustive theory or philosophy of the nature of manhood in all the range I have indicated. I am here to speak to you of a peculiar type of manhood under the title of

SELF-MADE MEN.

That there is, in more respects than one, something like a solecism in this title, I freely admit. Properly speaking, there are in the world no such men as self-made men. That term implies an individual independence of the past and present which can never exist.

Our best and most valued acquisitions have been obtained either from our contemporaries or from those who have preceded us in the field of thought and discovery. We have all either begged, borrowed or stolen. We have reaped where others have sown, and that which others have strown, we have gathered. It must in truth be said though it may not accord well with self-conscious individuality and self-conceit, that no possible native force of character, and no depth or wealth of originality, can lift a man into absolute independence of his fellow men, and no generation of men can be independent of the preceding generation. The brotherhood and inter-dependence of mankind are guarded and defended at all points. I believe in individuality, but individuals are, to the mass, like waves to the ocean. The highest order of genius is as dependent as is the lowest. It, like the loftiest waves of the sea, derives its power and greatness from the grandeur and vastness of the ocean of which it forms a part. We differ as the waves, but are one as the sea. To do something well does not necessarily imply the ability to do everything else equally well. If you can do in one direction that which I cannot do, I may in another direction, be able to do that which you cannot do. Thus the balance of power is kept comparatively even, and a self-acting brotherhood and inter-dependence is maintained.

Nevertheless, the title of my lecture is eminently descriptive of a class and is, moreover, a fit and convenient one for my purpose, in illustrating the idea which I have in view. In the order of discussion I shall adopt the style of an old-fashioned preacher and have a "firstly," a "secondly," a "thirdly," a "fourthly" and, possibly, a "conclusion."

My first is, "Who are self-made men?" My second is, "What is the true theory of their success?" My third is, "The advantages which self-made men derive from the manners and institutions of their surroundings," and my fourth is, "The grounds of the criticism to which they are, as a class, especially exposed."

On the first point I may say that, by the term "self-made men," I mean especially what, to the popular mind, the term itself imports. Self-made men are the men who, under peculiar difficulties and without the ordinary helps of favoring circumstances, have attained knowledge, usefulness, power and position and have learned from themselves the best uses to which life can be put in this world, and in the exercises of these uses to build up worthy character. They are the men who owe little or nothing to birth, relationship, friendly surroundings; to wealth inherited or to early approved means of education; who are what they are, without the aid of any of the favoring conditions by which other men usually rise in the world and achieve great results. In fact they are the men who are not brought up but who are obliged to come up, not only without the voluntary assistance or friendly cooperation of society, but often in open and derisive defiance of all the efforts of society and the tendency of circumstances to repress, retard and keep them down. They are the men who, in a world of schools, academies, colleges and other institutions of learning, are often compelled by unfriendly circumstances to acquire their education elsewhere and, amidst unfavorable conditions, to hew out for themselves a way to success, and thus to become the architects of their own good fortunes. They are in a peculiar sense, indebted to themselves for themselves. If they have traveled far, they have made the road on which they traveled. If they have ascended high, they have built their own ladder. From the depths of poverty such as these have often come. From the heartless pavements of large and crowded cities; barefooted, homeless, and friendless, they have come. From hunger, rags and destitution, they have come; motherless and fatherless, they have come, and may come. Flung overboard in the midnight storm on the broad and tempest-tossed ocean of life; left without ropes, planks, oars or life-preservers, they have bravely buffetted the frowning billows and have risen in safety and life where others, supplied with the best appliances for safety and success, have fainted, despaired and gone down forever.

Such men as these, whether found in one position or another, whether in the college or in the factory; whether professors or plowmen; whether Caucasian or Indian; whether Anglo-Saxon or Anglo-African, are self-made men and are entitled to a certain measure of respect for their success and for proving to the world the grandest possibilities of human nature, of whatever variety of race or color.

Though a man of this class need not claim to be a hero or to be worshiped as such, there is genuine heroism in his struggle and something of sublimity and glory in his triumph. Every instance of such success is an example and a help to humanity. It, better than any mere assertion, gives us assurance of the latent powers and resources of simple and unaided manhood. It dignifies labor, honors application, lessens pain and depression, dispels gloom from the brow of the destitute and weariness from the heart of him about to faint, and enables man to take hold of the roughest and flintiest hardships incident to the battle of life, with a lighter heart, with higher hopes and a larger courage.

But I come at once to the second part of my subject, which respects the

THEORY OF SELF-MADE MEN.

"Upon what meat doth this, our CÆSAR, feed, he hath grown so great?" How happens it that the cottager is often found equal to the lord, and that, in the race of life, the sons of the poor often get even with, and surpass even, the sons of the rich? How happens it from the

field often come statesmen equal to those from the college? I am sorry
to say that, upon this interesting point, I can promise nothing absolute nor anything which will be entirely satisfactory and conclusive.
Burns says:

> "I see how folks live that hae riches,
> But surely poor folks maun be witches."

The various conditions of men and the different uses they make of
their powers and opportunities in life, are full of puzzling contrasts and
contradictions. Here, as elsewhere, it is easy to dogmatize, but it is not
so easy to define, explain and demonstrate. The natural laws for the
government, well-being and progress of mankind, seem to be equal
and are equal; but the subjects of these laws everywhere abound in in-
equalities, discords and contrasts. We cannot have fruit without flowers,
but we often have flowers without fruit. The promise of youth often
breaks down in manhood, and real excellence often comes unheralded
and from unexpected quarters.

The scene presented from this view is as a thousand arrows shot from
the same point and aimed at the same object. United in aim, they are
divided in flight. Some fly too high, others too low. Some go to the
right, others to the left. Some fly too far and others, not far enough, and
only a few hit the mark. Such is life. United in the quiver, they are divided in the air. Matched when dormant, they are unmatched in action.

When we attempt to account for greatness we never get nearer to
the truth than did the greatest of poets and philosophers when he classified the conditions of greatness: "Some are born great, some achieve
greatness and some have greatness thrust upon them." We may take our
choice of these three separate explanations and make which of them
we please, most prominent in our discussion. Much can certainly be
said of superior mental endowments, and I should on some accounts,
lean strongly to that theory, but for numerous examples which seem to,
and do, contradict it, and but for the depressing tendency such a theory
must have upon humanity generally.

This theory has truth in it, but it is not the whole truth. Men of
very ordinary faculties have, nevertheless, made a very respectable way
in the world and have sometimes presented even brilliant examples of
success. On the other hand, what is called genius is often found by the
wayside, a miserable wreck; the more deplorable and shocking because
from the height from which it has fallen and the loss and ruin involved
in the fall. There is, perhaps, a compensation in disappointment and in
the contradiction of means to ends and promise to performance. These
imply a constant effort on the part of nature to hold the balance evenly

between all her children and to bring success within the reach of the humblest as well as of the most exalted.

From apparently the basest metals we have the finest toned bells, and we are taught respect from simple manhood when we see how, from the various dregs of society, there come men who may well be regarded as the pride and as the watch towers of the race.

Steel is improved by laying on damp ground, and the rusty razor gets a keener edge after giving its dross to the dirt in which it has been allowed to lie neglected and forgotten. In like manner, too, humanity, though it lay among the pots, covered with the dust of neglect and poverty, may still retain the divine impulse and the element of improvement and progress. It is natural to revolt at squalor, but we may well relax our lip of scorn and contempt when we stand among the lowly and despised, for out of the rags of the meanest cradle there may come a great man and this is a treasure richer than all the wealth of the Orient.

I do not think much of the accident or good luck theory of self-made men. It is worth but little attention and has no practical value. An apple carelessly flung into a crowd may hit one person, or it may hit another, or it may hit nobody. The probabilities are precisely the same in this accident theory of self-made men. It divorces a man from his own achievements, contemplates him as a being of chance and leaves him without will, motive, ambition and aspiration. Yet the accident theory is among the most popular theories of individual success. It has about it the air of mystery which the multitude so well like, and withal, it does something to mar the complacency of the successful.

It is one of the easiest and commonest things in the world for a successful man to be followed in his career through life and to have constantly pointed out this or that particular stroke of good fortune which fixed his destiny and made him successful. If not ourselves great, we like to explain why others are so. We are stingy in our praise to merit, but generous in our praise to chance. Besides, a man feels himself measurably great when he can point out the precise moment and circumstance which made his neighbor great. He easily fancies that the slight difference between himself and his friend is simply one of luck. It was his friend who was lucky but it might easily have been himself. Then too, the next best thing to success is a valid apology for non-success. Detraction is, to many, a delicious morsel. The excellence which it loudly denies to others it silently claims for itself. It possesses the means of covering the small with the glory of the great. It adds to failure that which it takes from success and shortens the distance between those in front and those in the rear. Even here there is an upward tendency worthy of notice and respect. The kitchen is ever the critic of the parlor. The talk of those below is of those above. We imitate those we revere and admire.

But the main objection to this very comfortable theory is that, like most other theories, it is made to explain too much. While it ascribes success to chance and friendly circumstances, it is apt to take no cognizance of the very different uses to which different men put their circumstances and their chances.

Fortune may crowd a man's life with favorable circumstances and happy opportunities, but they will, as all know, avail him nothing unless he makes a wise and vigorous use of them. It does not matter that the wind is fair and the tide at its flood, if the mariner refuses to weigh his anchor and spread his canvas to the breeze. The golden harvest is ripe in vain if the farmer refuses to reap. Opportunity is important but exertion is indispensable. "There is a tide in the affairs of men which, taken at its flood, leads on to fortune;" but it must be taken at its flood.

Within this realm of man's being, as elsewhere, Science is diffusing its broad, beneficent light. As this light increases, dependence upon chance or luck is destined to vanish and the wisdom of adapting means to ends, to become more manifest.

It was once more common than it is now, to hear men religiously ascribing their good or ill fortune directly to supernatural intervention. Success and failure, wealth and poverty, intelligence and ignorance, liberty and slavery, happiness and misery, were all bestowed or inflicted upon individual men by a divine hand and for all-wise purposes. Man was, by such reasoners, made a very insignificant agent in his own affairs. It was all the Lord's doings and marvellous to human eyes. Of course along with this superstition came the fortune teller, the pretender to divination and the miracle working priest who could save from famine by praying easier than by under-draining and deep plowing.

In such matter a wise man has little use for altars or oracle. He knows that the laws of God are perfect and unchangeable. He knows that health is maintained by right living; that disease is cured by the right use of remedies; that bread is produced by tilling the soil; that knowledge is obtained by study; that wealth is secured by saving and that battles are won by fighting. To him, the lazy man is the unlucky man and the man of luck is the man of work.

> "The fault, dear Brutus, is not in our stars,
> But in ourselves, that we are underlings."

When we find a man who has ascended heights beyond ourselves; who has a broader range of vision than we and a sky with more stars in it than we have in ours, we may know that he has worked harder, better and more wisely than we. He was awake while we slept. He was busy while we were idle and he was wisely improving his time and talents while we were wasting ours. Paul Dunbar, the colored poet, has well said:

"There are no beaten paths to glory's height,
There are no rules to compass greatness known;
Each for himself must cleave a path alone,
And press his own way forward in the fight.
Smooth is the way to ease and calm delight,
And soft the road Sloth chooseth for her own;
But he who craves the flow'r of life full-blown
Must struggle up in all his armor dight.
What tho' the burden bear him sorely down,
And crush to dust the mountain of his pride.
Oh! then with strong heart let him still abide
For rugged is the road way to renown.
Nor may he hope to gain the envied crown
Till he hath thrust the looming rocks aside."

I am certain that there is nothing good, great or desirable which man can possess in this world, that does not come by some kind of labor, either physical or mental, moral or spiritual. A man may, at times, get something for nothing, but it will, in his hands, amount to nothing. What is true in the world of matter, is equally true in the world of mind. Without culture there can be no growth; without exertion, no acquisition; without friction, no polish; without labor, no knowledge; without action, no progress and without conflict, no victory. The man who lies down a fool at night, hoping that he will waken wise in the morning, will rise up in the morning as he laid down in the evening.

Faith, in the absence of work, seems to be worth little, if anything. The preacher who finds it easier to pray for knowledge than to tax his brain with study and application will find his congregation growing beautifully less and his flock looking elsewhere for their spiritual and mental food. In the old slave times colored ministers were somewhat remarkable for the fervor with which they prayed for knowledge, but it did not appear that they were remarkable for any wonderful success. In fact, they who prayed loudest seemed to get least. They thought if they opened their mouths they would be filled. The result was an abundance of sound with a great destitution of sense.

Not only in man's experience, but also in nature do we find exemplified the truth upon which I have been insisting. My father worketh, said the Savior, and I also work. In every view which we obtain of the perfections of the universe; whether we look to the bright stars in the peaceful blue dome above us, or to the long shore line of the ocean, where land and water maintain eternal conflict; the lesson taught is the same; that of endless action and reaction. Those beautifully rounded pebbles which you gather on the sand and which you hold in your hand and marvel at their exceeding smoothness, were chiseled into their varied and graceful forms by the ceaseless action of countless waves. Nature is herself a great worker and never tolerates, without certain rebuke, any contradiction to her wise example. Inaction is followed by stagnation. Stagnation is followed by pestilence and pestilence is followed by death. General Butler, busy with his broom, could sweep yellow fever out of New Orleans, but this dread destroyer returned when the General and his broom were withdrawn, and the people, neglecting sanitary wisdom, went on ascribing to Divinity what was simply due to dirt.

From these remarks it will be evident that, allowing only ordinary ability and opportunity, we may explain success mainly by one word and that word is WORK! WORK!! WORK!!! WORK!!!! Not transient and fitful effort, but patient, enduring, honest, unremitting and indefatigable work, into which the whole heart is put, and which, in both temporal and spiritual affairs, is the true miracle worker. Every one may avail himself of this marvellous power, if he will. There is no royal road to perfection. Certainly no one must wait for some kind friend to put a springing board under his feet, upon which he may easily bound from the first round of the ladder onward and upward to its highest round. If he waits for this, he may wait long and perhaps forever. He who does not think himself worth saving from poverty and ignorance, by his own efforts, will hardly be thought worth the efforts of anybody else.

The lesson taught at this point by human experience is simply this, that the man who will get up will be helped up; and that the man who will not get up will be allowed to stay down. This rule may appear somewhat harsh, but in its general application and operation it is wise, just and beneficent. I know of no other rule which can be substituted for it without bringing social chaos. Personal independence is a virtue and it is the soul out of which comes the sturdiest manhood. But there can be no independence without a large share of self-dependence, and this virtue cannot be bestowed. It must be developed from within.

I have been asked "How will this theory affect the Negro?" and "What shall be done in his case?" My general answer is "Give the Negro fair play and let him alone. If he lives, well. If he dies, equally well. If he cannot stand up, let him fall down."

The apple must have strength and vitality enough in itself to hold on, or it will fall to the ground where it belongs. The strongest influence prevails and should prevail. If the vital relation of the fruit is severed, it is folly to tie the stem to the branch or the branch to the tree or to shelter the fruit from the wind. So, too, there is no wisdom in lifting from the earth a head which must only fall the more heavily when the help is withdrawn. Do right, though the heavens fall; but they will not fall.

I have said "Give the Negro fair play and let him alone." I meant all that I said and a good deal more than some understand by fair play. It is not fair play to start the Negro out in life, from nothing and with nothing, while others start with the advantage of a thousand years behind them. He should be measured, not by the heights others have obtained, but from the depths from which he has come. For any adjustment of the seals of comparison, fair play demands that to the barbarism from which the Negro started shall be added two hundred years heavy with human bondage. Should the American people put a school house in every valley of the South and a church on every hill side and supply the one with teachers and the other with preachers, for a hundred years to come, they would not then have given fair play to the Negro.

The nearest approach to justice to the Negro for the past is to do him justice in the present. Throw open to him the doors of the schools, the factories, the workshops, and of all mechanical industries. For his own welfare, give him a chance to do whatever he can do well. If he fails then, let him fail! I can, however, assure you that he will not fail. Already has he proven it. As a soldier he proved it. He has since proved it by industry and sobriety and by the acquisition of knowledge and property. He is almost the only successful tiller of the soil of the South, and is fast becoming the owner of land formerly owned by his old master and by the old master class. In a thousand instances has he verified my theory of self-made men. He well performed the task of making bricks without straw: now give him straw. Give him all the facilities for honest and successful livelihood, and in all honorable avocations receive him as a man among men.

I have by implication admitted that work alone is not the only explanation of self-made men, or of the secret of success. Industry, to be sure, is the superficial and visible cause of success, but what is the cause of industry? In the answer to this question one element is easily pointed out, and that element is necessity. Thackeray very wisely remarks that "All men are about as lazy as they can afford to be." Men cannot be depended upon to work when they are asked to work for nothing. They are not only as lazy as they can afford to be, but I have found many who were a great deal more so. We all hate the task master, but all men, however industrious, are either lured or lashed through the world, and we should be a lazy, good-for-nothing set, if we were not so lured and lashed.

Necessity is not only the mother of invention, but the mainspring of exertion. The presence of some urgent, pinching, imperious necessity, will often not only sting a man into marvellous exertion, but into a sense of the possession, within himself, of powers and resources which else had slumbered on through a long life, unknown to himself and never suspected by others. A man never knows the strength of his grip till life and limb depend upon it. Something is likely to be done when something must be done.

If you wish to make your son helpless, you need not cripple him with bullet or bludgeon, but simply place him beyond the reach of necessity and surround him with ease and luxury. This experiment has often been tried and has seldom failed. As a general rule, where circumstances do most for men, there man will do least for himself; and where man does least, he himself is least. His doing or not doing makes or unmakes him.

Under the palm trees of Africa man finds, without effort, food, raiment and shelter. For him, there, Nature has done all and he has done nothing. The result is that the glory of Africa is in her palms,—and not in her men.

In your search after manhood go not to those delightful latitudes where "summer is blossoming all the year long," but rather to the hardy North, to Maine, New Hampshire and Vermont, to the coldest and flintiest parts of New England, where men work gardens with gunpowder, blast rocks to find places to plant potatoes; where, for six months of the year, the earth is covered with snow and ice. Go to the states which Daniel Webster thought good enough to emigrate from, and there you will find the highest type of American physical and intellectual manhood.

Happily for mankind, labor not only supplies the good things for which it is exerted, but it increases its own resources and improves, sharpens and strengthens its own instruments.

The primary condition upon which men have and retain power and skill is exertion. Nature has no use for unused power. She abhors a vacuum. She permits no preemption without occupation. Every organ of body and mind has its use and improves by use. "Better to wear out than to rust out," is sound philosophy as well as common sense. The eye of the watch-maker is severely taxed by the intense light and effort necessary in order to see minute objects, yet it remains clear and keen long after those of other men have failed. I was told at the Remington Rifle Works, by the workmen there employed who have to straighten the rifle barrels by flashing intense light through them, that, by this practice, severe as it seems, their eyes were made stronger.

But what the hands find to do must be done in earnest. Nature tolerates no halfness. He who wants hard hands must not, at sight of the first blister, fling away the spade, the rake, the broad axe or the hoe; for the blister is a primary condition to the needed hardness. To abandon work is not only to throw away the means of success, but it is also to part with the ability to work. To be able to walk well, one must walk on, and to work with ease and effect, one must work on.

Thus the law of labor is self-acting, beneficent and perfect; increasing skill and ability according to exertion. Faithful, earnest and protracted industry gives strength to the mind and facility to the hand. Within certain limits, the more that a man does, the more he can do.

Few men ever reach, in any one direction, the limits of their possibilities. As in commerce, so here, the relation of supply to demand rules. Our mechanical and intellectual forces increase or decrease according to the demands made upon them. He who uses most will have most to use. This is the philosophy of the parable of the ten talents. It applies here as elsewhere. "To him that hath shall be given and from him that hath not shall be taken even that which he hath."

Exertion of muscle or mind, for pleasure and amusement alone, cannot bring anything like the good results of earnest labor. Such exertion lacks the element attached to duty. To play perfectly upon any complicated instrument, one must play long, laboriously and with earnest purpose. Though it be an amusement at first, it must be labor at the end, if any proficiency is reached. If one plays for one's own pleasure alone, the performance will give little pleasure to any one else and will finally become a rather hard and dry pleasure to one's self.

In this respect one cannot receive much more than one gives. Men may cheat their neighbors and may cheat themselves but they cannot cheat nature. She will only pay the wages one honestly earns.

In the idea of exertion, of course fortitude and perseverance are included. We have all met a class of men, very remarkable for their activity, and who yet make but little headway in life; men who, in their noisy and impulsive pursuit of knowledge, never get beyond the outer bark of an idea, from a lack of patience and perseverance to dig to the core; men who begin everything and complete nothing; who see, but do not perceive; who read, but forget what they read, and are as if they had not read; who travel, but go nowhere in particular, and have nothing of value to impart when they return. Such men may have greatness thrust upon them but they never achieve greatness.

As the gold in the mountain is concealed in huge and flinty rocks, so the most valuable ideas and inventions are often enveloped in doubt and uncertainty. The printing press, the sewing machine, the railroad, the telegraph and the locomotive, are all simple enough now, but who can measure the patience, the persistence, the fortitude, the wearing labor and the brain sweat, which produced these wonderful and indispensable additions to our modern civilization.

My theory of self-made men is, then, simply this; that they are men of work. Whether or not such men have acquired material, moral or intellectual excellence, honest labor faithfully, steadily and persistently pursued, is the best, if not the only, explanation of their success. But in thus awarding praise to industry, as the main agency in the production and culture of self-made men, I do not exclude other factors of the problem. I only make them subordinate. Other agencies cooperate, but this is the principal one and the one without which all others would fail.

Indolence and failure can give a thousand excuses for themselves. How often do we hear men say, "If I had the head of this one, or the hands of that one; the health of this one, or the strength of that one; the chances of this or of that one, I might have been this, that, or the other"; and much more of the same sort.

Sound bodily health and mental faculties unimpaired are very desirable, if not absolutely indispensable. But a man need not be a physical giant or an intellectual prodigy, in order to make a tolerable way in the world. The health and strength of the soul is of far more importance than is that of the body, even when viewed as a means of mundane results. The soul is the main thing. Man can do a great many things; some easily and some with difficulty, but he cannot build a sound ship with rotten timber. Her model may be faultless; her spars may be the finest and her canvas the whitest and the flags of all nations may be displayed at her masthead, but she will go down in the first storm. So it is with the soul. Whatever its assumptions, if it be lacking in the principles of honor, integrity and affection, it, too, will go down in the first storm. And when the soul is lost, all is lost. All human experience proves over and over again, that any success which comes through meanness, trickery, fraud and dishonor, is but emptiness and will only be a torment to its possessor.

Let not the morally strong, though physically weak abandon the struggle of life. For such happily, there is both place and chance in the world. The highest services to man and the richest rewards to the worker are not conditioned entirely upon physical power. The higher the plane of civilization, the more abundant the opportunities of the weak and infirm. Society and civilization move according to celestial order. "Not that which is spiritual is first, but that which is natural. After that, that which is spiritual." The order of progress, is, first, barbarism; afterward, civilization. Barbarism represents physical force. Civilization represents spiritual power. The primary condition, that of barbarism, knows no other law than that of force; not right, but might. In this condition of society, or rather of no society, the man of mind is pushed aside by the man of muscle. A Kit Carson, far out on the borders of civilization, dexterously handling his bowie knife, rifle and bludgeon, easily gets himself taken for a hero; but the waves of science and civilization rolling out over the Western prairies, soon leave him no room for his barbarous accomplishment. Kit is shorn of his glory. A higher type of manhood is required.

Where ferocious beasts and savage inhabitants have been dispersed and the rudeness of nature has been subdued, we welcome milder methods and gentler instrumentalities for the service of mankind. Here the race is not to the swift nor the battle to the strong, but the prize is brought within the reach of those who are neither swift nor strong. None need despair. There is room and work for all: for the weak as well as the strong. Activity is the law for all and its rewards are open to all. Vast acquirements and splendid achievements stand to the credit of men of feeble frames and slender constitutions. Channing was physically weak. Milton was blind. Montgomery was small and effeminate. But these men were more to the world than a thousand Sampsons. Mrs Stowe would be nothing among the grizzly bears of the Rocky mountains. We should not be likely to ask for her help at a barn raising, or a ship launch; but when a great national evil was to be removed; when a nation's heart was to be touched; when a whole country was to be redeemed and regenerated and millions of slaves converted into free men, the civilized world knew no earthly power equal to hers.

But another element of the secret of success demands a word. That element is order, systematic endeavor. We succeed, not alone by the laborious exertion of our faculties, be they small or great, but by the regular, thoughtful and systematic exercise of them. Order, the first law of heaven, is itself a power. The battle is nearly lost when your lines are in disorder. Regular, orderly and systematic effort which moves without friction and needless loss of time or power; which has a place for everything and everything in its place; which knows just where to begin, how to proceed and where to end, though marked by no extraordinary outlay of energy or activity, will work wonders, not only in the matter of accomplishment, but also in the increase of the ability of the individual. It will make the weak man strong and the strong man stronger; the simple man wise and the wise man, wiser, and will insure success by the power and influence that belong to habit.

On the other hand, no matter what gifts and what aptitudes a man may possess; no matter though his mind be of the highest order and fitted for the noblest achievements; yet, without this systematic effort, his genius will only serve as a fire of shavings, soon in blaze and soon out.

Spontaneity has a special charm, and the fitful outcroppings of genius are, in speech or action, delightful; but the success attained by these is neither solid nor lasting. A man who, for nearly forty years, was the foremost orator in New England, was asked by me, if his speeches were extemporaneous? They flowed so smoothly that I had my doubts about it. He answered, "No, I carefully think out and write my speeches, before I utter them." When such a man rises to speak, he knows what he is going to say. When he speaks, he knows what he is saying. When he retires from the platform, he knows what he *has* said.

There is still another element essential to success, and that is, a commanding object and a sense of its importance. The vigor of the action depends upon the power of the motive. The wheels of the locomotive lie idle upon the rail until they feel the impelling force of the steam; but when that is applied, the whole ponderous train is set in motion. But energy ought not to be wasted. A man may dispose of his life as Paddy did of his powder,—aim at nothing, and hit it every time.

If each man in the world did his share of honest work, we should have no need of a millennium. The world would teem with abundance, and the temptation to evil in a thousand directions, would disappear. But work is not often undertaken for its own sake. The worker is conscious of an object worthy of effort, and works for that object; not for what he is to it, but for what it is to him. All are not moved by the same objects. Happiness is the object of some. Wealth and fame are the objects of others. But wealth and fame are beyond the reach of the majority of men, and thus, to them, these are not motive-impelling objects. Happily, however, personal, family and neighborhood well-being stand near to us all and are full of lofty inspirations to earnest endeavor, if we would but respond to their influence.

I do not desire my lecture to become a sermon; but, were this allowable, I would rebuke the growing tendency to sport and pleasure. The time, money and strength devoted to these phantoms, would banish darkness and hunger from every hearthstone in our land. Multitudes, unconscious of any controlling object in life, flit, like birds, from point to point; now here, now there; and so accomplish nothing, either here or there.

"For pleasures are like poppies spread,
You seize the flower, its bloom is shed!
Or like the snow-falls in the river,
A moment white—then melts forever;
Or like the borealis race,
That flit ere you can point their place;
Or like the rainbow's lovely form
Evanishing amid the storm.—"

They know most of pleasure who seek it least, and they least who seek it most. The cushion is soft to him who sits on it but seldom. The men behind the chairs at Saratoga and Newport, get better dinners than the men in them. We cannot serve two masters. When here, we cannot be there. If we accept ease, we must part with appetite. A pound of feathers is as heavy as a pound of iron,—and about as hard, if you sit on it long enough. Music is delightful, but too much of it wounds the ear like the filing of a saw. The lounge, to the lazy, becomes like flint; and to him, the most savory dishes lose their flavor.

> "It's true, they need na starve or sweat,
> Thro' winter's cauld or simmer's heat;
> But human bodies are sic fools,
> For all their colleges an' schools,
> That when na real ills perplex them,
> They make now, themselves to vex them."

But the industrious man does find real pleasure. He finds it in qualities and quantities to which the baffled pleasure seeker is a perpetual stranger. He finds it in the house well built, in the farm well tilled, in the books well kept, in the page well written, in the thought well expressed, in all the improved conditions of life around him and in whatsoever useful work may, for the moment, engage his time and energies.

I will give you, in one simple statement, my idea, my observation and my experience of the chief agent in the success of self-made men. It is not luck, nor is it great mental endowments, but it is well directed, honest toil. "Toil and Trust!" was the motto of John Quincy Adams, and his Presidency of the Republic proved its wisdom as well as its truth. Great in his opportunities, great in his mental endowments and great in his relationships, he was still greater in persevering and indefatigable industry.

Examples of successful self-culture and self-help under great difficulties and discouragements, are abundant, and they vindicate the theory of success thus feebly and with homely common sense, presented. For example: Hugh Miller, whose lamented death mantled the mountains and valleys of his native land with a broad shadow of sorrow, scarcely yet lifted, was a grand example of the success of persistent devotion, under great difficulties, to work and to the acquisition of knowledge. In a country justly distinguished for its schools and colleges, he, like Robert Burns, Scotia's matchless son of song, was the true child of science, as Burns was of song. He was his own college. The earth was his school and the rocks were his school master. Outside of all the learned institutions of his country, and while employed with his chisel and hammer, as a stone mason, this man literally killed two birds with one stone; for he earned his daily bread and at the same time made himself an eminent geologist, and gave to the world books which are found in all public libraries and which are full of inspiration to the truth seeker.

Not unlike the case of Hugh Miller, is that of our own Elihu Burritt. The true heart warms with admiration for the energy and perseverance displayed in this man's pursuit of knowledge. We call him "The learned blacksmith," and the distinction was fairly earned and fitly worn. Over the polished anvil and glowing forge; amidst the smoke, dust and din of the blacksmith's shop; amidst its blazing fires and hissing sparks, and while hammering the red-hot steel, this brave son of toil is said to have mastered twenty different languages, living and dead.

It is surprising with what small means, in the field of earnest effort, great results have been achieved. That neither costly apparatus nor packed libraries are necessarily required by the earnest student in self-culture, was demonstrated in a remarkable manner by Louis Kossuth. That illustrious patriot, scholar and statesman, came to our country from the far east of Europe, a complete master of the English language. He spoke our difficult tongue with an eloquence as stately and grand as that of the best American orators. When asked how he obtained this mastery of a language so foreign to him, he told us that his school house was an Austrian prison, and his school books, the Bible, Shakespeare, and an old English dictionary.

Side by side with the great Hungarian, let me name the King of American self-made men; the man who rose highest and will be remembered longest as the most popular and beloved President since Washington—ABRAHAM LINCOLN. This man came to us, not from the schools or from the mansions of ease and luxury, but from the back woods. He mastered his grammar by the light of a pine wood torch. The fortitude and industry which could split rails by day, and learn grammar at night at the hearthstone of a log but and by the unsteady glare of a pine wood knot, prepared this man for a service to his country and to mankind, which only the most exalted could have performed.

The examples thus far given, belong to the Caucassian race; but to the African race, as well, we are indebted for examples equally worthy and inspiring. Benjamin Bannecker, a man of African descent, born and reared in the state of Maryland, and a contemporary with the great men of the revolution, is worthy to be mentioned with the highest of his class. He was a slave, withheld from all those inspiring motives which freedom, honor and distinction furnish to exertion; and yet this man secured an English education; became a learned mathematician, was an excellent surveyor, assisted to lay out the city of Washington, and compelled honorable recognition from some of the most distinguished scholars and statesmen of that early day of the Republic.

The intellect of the Negro was then, as now, the subject of learned inquiry. Mr. Jefferson, among other statesmen and philosophers, while he considered slavery an evil, entertained a rather low estimate of the Negro's mental ability. He thought that the Negro might become learned in music and in language, but that mathematics were quite out of the question with him.

In this debate Benjamin Bannecker came upon the scene and materially assisted in lifting his race to a higher consideration than that in which it had been previously held. Bannecker was not only proficient as a writer, but, like Jefferson, he was a philosopher. Hearing of Mr. Jefferson's opinion of Negro intellect, he took no offense but calmly addressed that statesman a letter and a copy of an almanac for which he had made the astronomical calculations. The reply of Mr. Jefferson is the highest praise I wish to bestow upon this black self-made man. It is brief and I take great pleasure in presenting it.

PHILADELPHIA, August 30, 1790.

SIR:

I thank you sincerely for your letter and the almanac it contains. Nobody more than I do, wishes to see such proofs as you exhibit, that nature has given our black brethren talents equal to those of other colors of men, and that the appearance of the want of them, is owing mainly to the degrading conditions of their existence in Africa and America. I have taken the liberty of sending your almanac to Monsieur Cordozett, Secretary of the Academy of Science at Paris, and a member of the Philanthropic Society, because I considered it a document of which your whole race had a right, for their justification against the doubts entertained of them.

I am, with great esteem, sir,
Your most obedient servant,
THOMAS JEFFERSON.

This was the impression made by an intelligent Negro upon the father of American Democracy, in the earlier and better years of the Republic. I wish that it were possible to make a similar impression upon the children of the American Democracy of this generation. Jefferson was not ashamed to call the black man his brother and to address him as a gentleman.

I am sorry that Bannecker was not entirely black, because in the United States, the slightest infusion of Teutonic blood is thought to be sufficient to account for any considerable degree of intelligence found under any possible color of the skin.

But Bannecker is not the only colored example that I can give. While I turn with honest pride to Bannecker, who lived a hundred years ago, and invoke his aid to roll back the tide of disparagement and contempt which pride and prejudice have poured out against the colored race, I can also cite examples of like energy in our own day.

William Dietz, a black man of Albany, New York, with whom I was personally acquainted and of whom I can speak from actual knowledge, is one such. This man by industry, fidelity and general aptitude for business affairs, rose from the humble calling of house servant in the Dudley family of that city, to become the sole manager of the family estate valued at three millions of dollars.

It is customary to assert that the Negro never invented anything, and that, if he were today struck out of life, there would, in twenty years, be nothing left to tell of his existence. Well, this black man; for he was positively and perfectly black; not partially, but WHOLLY black; a man whom, a few years ago, some of our learned ethnologists would have read out of the human family and whom a certain Chief Justice would have turned out of court as a creature having no rights which white men are bound to respect, was one of the very best draftsmen and designers in the state of New York. Mr. Dietz was not only an architect, but he was also an inventor. In this he was a direct contradiction to the maligners of his race. The noble railroad bridge now spanning the Hudson river at Albany, was, in all essential features, designed by William Dietz. The main objection against a bridge across that highway of commerce had been that of its interference with navigation. Of all the designs presented, that of Dietz was the least objectionable on that score, and was, in its essential features, accepted. Mr. Dietz also devised a plan for an elevated railway to be built in Broadway, New York. The great objection to a railway in that famous thoroughfare was then, as now, that of the noise, dust, smoke, obstruction and danger to life and limb, thereby involved. Dietz undertook to remove all these objections by suggesting an elevated railway, the plan of which was, at the time, published in the *Scientific American* and highly commended by the editor of that journal. The then readers of the *Scientific American* read this account of the inventions of William Dietz, but did not know, as I did, that Mr. Dietz was a black man. There was certainly nothing in his name or in his works to suggest the American idea of color.

Among my dark examples I can name no man with more satisfaction than I can Toussaint L'Overture, the hero of Santo Domingo. Though born a slave and held a slave till he was fifty years of age; though, like Bannecker, he was black and showed no trace of Caucassian admixture, history hands him down to us as a brave and generous soldier, a wise and powerful statesmen, an ardent patriot and a successful liberator of his people and of his country.

The cotemporaries of this Haitien chief paint him as without a single moral blemish; while friends and foes alike, accord him the highest ability. In his eulogists no modern hero has been more fortunate than Toussaint L'Overture. History, poetry and eloquence have vied with each other to do him reverence. Wordsworth and Whittier have, in characteristic verse, encircled his brow with a halo of fadeless glory, while Phillips has borne him among the gods in something like Elijah's chariot of fire.

The testimony of these and a thousand others who have come up from depths of society, confirms the theory that industry is the most potent factor in the success of self-made men, and thus raises the dignity of labor; for whatever may be one's natural gifts, success, as I have said, is due mainly to this great means, open and free to all.

A word now upon the third point suggested at the beginning of this paper; namely, the friendly relation and influence of American ideas and institutions to this class of men.

America is said, and not without reason, to be preeminently the home and patron of self-made men. Here, all doors fly open to them. They may aspire to any position. Courts, Senates and Cabinets, spread rich carpets for their feet, and they stand among our foremost men in every honorable service. Many causes have made it easy, here, for this class to rise and flourish, and first among these causes is the general respectability of labor. Search where you will, there is no country on the globe where labor is so respected and the laborer so honored, as in this country. The conditions in which American society originated; the free spirit which framed its independence and created its government based upon the will of the people, exalted both labor and laborer. The strife between capital and labor is, here, comparatively equal. The one is not the haughty and powerful master and the other the weak and abject slave as is the case in some parts of Europe. Here, the man of toil is not bowed, but erect and strong. He feels that capital is not more indispensable than labor, and he can therefore meet the capitalist as the representative of an equal power.

Of course these remarks are not intended to apply to the states where slavery has but recently existed. That system was the extreme degradation of labor, and though happily now abolished its consequences still linger and may not disappear for a century. To-day, in the presence of the capitalist, the Southern black laborer stands abashed, confused and intimidated. He is compelled to beg his fellow worm to give him leave to toil. Labor can never be respected where the laborer is despised. This is today, the great trouble at the South. The land owners still resent emancipation and oppose the elevation of labor. They have yet to learn that a condition of affairs well suited to a time of slavery may not be well suited to a time of freedom. They will one day learn that large farms and ignorant laborers are as little suited to the South as to the North.

But the respectability of labor is not, as already intimated, the only or the most powerful cause of the facility with which men rise from humble conditions to affluence and importance in the United States. A more subtle and powerful influence is exerted by the fact that the principle of measuring and valuing men according to their respective merits and without regard to their antecedents, is better established and more generally enforced here than in any other country. In Europe, greatness is often thrust upon men. They are made legislators by birth.

"A king can make a belted knight,
A marquis, duke and a' that."

But here, wealth and greatness are forced by no such capricious and arbitrary power. Equality of rights brings equality of positions and dignities. Here society very properly saves itself the trouble of looking up a man's kinsfolks in order to determine his grade in life and the measure of respect due him. It cares very little who was his father or grandfather. The boast of the Jews, "We have Abraham for our father," has no practical significance here. He who demands consideration on the strength of a reputation of a dead father, is, properly enough, rewarded with derision. We have no reverence to throw away in this wise.

As a people, we have only a decent respect for our seniors. We cannot be beguiled into accepting empty-headed sons for full-headed fathers. As some one has said, we dispense with the smoke when the candle is out. In popular phrase we exhort every man as he comes upon the stage of active life, "Now do your level best!" "Help yourself!" "Put your shoulder to the wheel!" "Make your own record!" "Paddle your own canoe!" "Be the architect of your own fortune!"

The sons of illustrious men are put upon trial like the sons of common people. They must prove themselves real CLAYS, WEBSTERS and LINCOLNS, if they would attract to themselves the cordial respect and admiration generally awarded to their brilliant fathers. There is, here, no law of entail or primogeniture.

Our great men drop out from their various groups and circles of greatness as bright meteors vanish from the blue overhanging sky bearing away their own silvery light and leaving the places where they once shone so brightly, robed in darkness till relighted in turn by the glory of succeeding ones.

I would not assume that we are entirely devoid of affection for families and for great names. We have this feeling, but it is a feeling qualified and limited by the popular thought; a thought which springs from the heart of free institutions and is destined to grow stronger the longer these institutions shall endure. George Washington, Jr., or Andrew Jackson, Jr., stand no better chance of being future Presidents than do the sons of Smith or Jones, or the sons of anybody else.

We are in this, as Edmund Quincy once said of the rapping spirits, willing to have done with people when they are done with us. We reject living pretenders if they come only in the old clothes of the dead.

We have as a people no past and very little present, but a boundless and glorious future. With us, it is not so much what has been, or what is now, but what is to be in the good time coming. Our mottoes are "Look ahead!" and "Go ahead!", and especially the latter. Our moral atmosphere is full of the inspiration of hope and courage. Every man has his chance. If he cannot be President he can, at least, be prosperous. In this respect, America is not only the exception to the general rule, but the social wonder of the world. Europe, with her divine-right governments and ultra-montane doctrines; with her sharply defined and firmly fixed classes; each class content if it can hold its own against the others, inspires little of individual hope or courage. Men, on all sides, endeavor to continue from youth to old age in their several callings and to abide in their several stations. They seldom hope for anything more or better than this. Once in a while, it is true, men of extraordinary energy and industry, like the Honorable John Bright and the Honorable Lord Brougham, (men whose capacity and disposition for work always left their associates little or nothing to do) rise even in England. Such men would rise to distinction anywhere. They do not disprove the general rule, but confirm it.

What is, in this respect, difficult and uncommon in the Old World, is quite easy and common in the New. To the people of Europe, this eager, ever moving mass which we call American society and in which life is not only a race, but a battle, and everybody trying to get just a little ahead of everybody else, looks very much like anarchy.

The remark is often made abroad that there is no repose in America. We are said to be like the troubled sea, and in some sense this is true. If it is a fact it is also one not without its compensation. If we resemble the sea in its troubles, we also resemble the sea in its power and grandeur, and in the equalities of its particles.

It is said, that in the course of centuries, I dare not say how many, all the oceans of this great globe go through the purifying process of filtration. All their parts are at work and their relations are ever changing. They are, in obedience to ever varying atmospheric forces, lifted from their lowly condition and are borne away by gentle winds or furious storms to far off islands, capes and continents; visiting in their course, mountain, valley and plain; thus fulfilling a beneficent mission and leaving the grateful earth refreshed, enriched, invigorated, beautiful and blooming. Each pearly drop has its fair chance to rise and contribute its share to the health and happiness of the world.

Such, in some sort, is a true picture of the restless activity and ever-changing relations of American society. Like the sea, we are constantly rising above, and returning to, the common level. A small son follows a great father, and a poor son, a rich father. To my mind we have no reason to fear that either wealth, knowledge or power will here be monopolized by the few as against the many.

These causes which make America the home and foster-mother of self-made men, combined with universal suffrage, will, I hope, preserve us from this danger. With equal suffrage in our hands, we are beyond the power of families, nationalities or races.

Then, too, our national genius welcomes humanity from every quarter and grants to all an equal chance in the race of life.

> "We ask not for his lineage,
> We ask not for his name;
> If manliness be in his heart,
> He noble birth may claim.
> We ask not from what land he came,
> Nor where his youth was nursed;
> If pure the stream, it matters not
> The spot from whence it burst."

Under the shadow of a great name, Louis Napoleon could strike down the liberties of France and erect the throne of a despot; but among a people so jealous of liberty as to revolt at the idea of electing, for a third term, one of our best Presidents, no such experiment as Napoleon's could ever be attempted here.

We are sometimes dazzled by the gilded show of aristocratic and monarchical institutions, and run wild to see a prince. We are willing that the nations which enjoy these superstitions and follies shall enjoy them in peace. But, for ourselves, we want none of them and will have none of them and can have none of them while the spirit of liberty and equality animates the Republic.

A word in conclusion, as to the criticisms and embarrassments to which self-made men are exposed, even in this highly favored country. A traveler through the monarchies of Europe is annoyed at every turn by a demand for his passport. Our government has imposed no such burden, either upon the traveler or upon itself. But citizens and private individuals, in their relation to each other and the world, demand of every one the equivalent of a passport to recognition, in the possession of some quality or acquirement which shall commend its possessor to favor. We believe in making ourselves pretty well acquainted with the character, business and history of all comers. We say to all such, "Stand and deliver!" And to this demand self-made men are especially subject.

There is a small class of very small men who turn their backs upon any one who presumes to be anybody, independent of Harvard, Yale, Princeton or other similar institutions of learning. These individuals cannot believe that any good can come out of Nazareth. With them, the diploma is more than the man. To that moral energy upon which depends the lifting of humanity, which is the world's true advancement, these are utter strangers. To them the world is never indebted for progress, and they may safely be left to the gentle oblivion which will surely overtake them.

By these remarks, however, there is meant no disparagement of learning. With all my admiration for self-made men, I am far from considering them the best made men. Their symmetry is often marred by the effects of their extra exertion. The hot rays of the sun and the long and rugged road over which they have been compelled to travel, have left their marks, sometimes quite visibly and unpleasantly, upon them.

While the world values skill and power, it values beauty and polish, as well. It was not alone the hard good sense and honest heart of Horace Greely, the self-made man, that made the *New York Tribune;* but likewise the brilliant and thoroughly educated men silently associated with him.

There never was a self-educated man, however well-educated, who, with the same exertion, would not have been better educated by the aid of schools and colleges. The charge is made and well sustained, that self-made men are not generally over modest or self-forgetful men. It was said of Horace Greeley, that he was a self-made man and worshipped his maker. Perhaps the strong resistance which such men meet in maintaining their claim, may account for much of their self-assertion.

The country knows by heart, and from his own lips, the story of Andrew Jackson. In many cases, the very energies employed, the obstacles overcome, the heights attained and the broad contrasts at every step forced upon the attention, tend to incite and strengthen egotism. A man indebted for himself to himself, may naturally think well of himself.

But this is apt to be far overdone. That a man has been able to make his own way in the world, is an humble fact as well as an honorable one. It is, however, possible to state a very humble fact in a very haughty manner, and self-made men are, as a class, much addicted to this habit. By this peculiarity they make themselves much less agreeable to society than they would otherwise be.

One other criticism upon these men is often very properly made. Having never enjoyed the benefits of schools, colleges and other like institutions of learning, they display for them a contempt which is quite ridiculous and which also makes them appear so. A man may know much about educating himself, and but little about the proper means for educating others. A self-made man is also liable to be full of contrarieties. He may be large, but at the same time, awkward; swift, but ungraceful; a man of power, but deficient in the polish and amiable proportions of the affluent and regularly educated man. I think that, generally, self-made men answer more or less closely to this description.

For practical benefit we are often about as much indebted to our enemies, as to our friends; as much to the men who hiss, as to those who applaud; for it may be with men as some one has said about tea; that if you wish to get its strength, you must put it into hot water. Criticism took Theodore Parker from a village pulpit and gave him the whole country for a platform and the whole nation for an audience. England laughed at American authorship and we sent her Emerson and Uncle Tom's Cabin. From its destitution of trees, Scotland was once a by-word; now it is a garden of beauty. Five generations ago, Britain was ashamed to write books in her own tongue. Now her language is spoken in all quarters of the globe. The Jim Crow Minstrels have, in many cases, led the Negro to the study of music; while the doubt cast upon the Negro's tongue has sent him to the lexicon and grammar and to the study of Greek orators and orations.

Thus detraction paves the way for the very perfections which it doubts and denies.

Ladies and gentlemen: Accept my thanks for your patient attention. I will detain you no longer. If, by statement, argument, sentiment or example, I have awakened in any, a sense of the dignity of labor or the value of manhood, or have stirred in any mind, a courageous resolution to make one more effort towards self-improvement and higher usefulness, I have not spoken altogether in vain, and your patience is justified.